You become like the 5 people you spend the most time with.

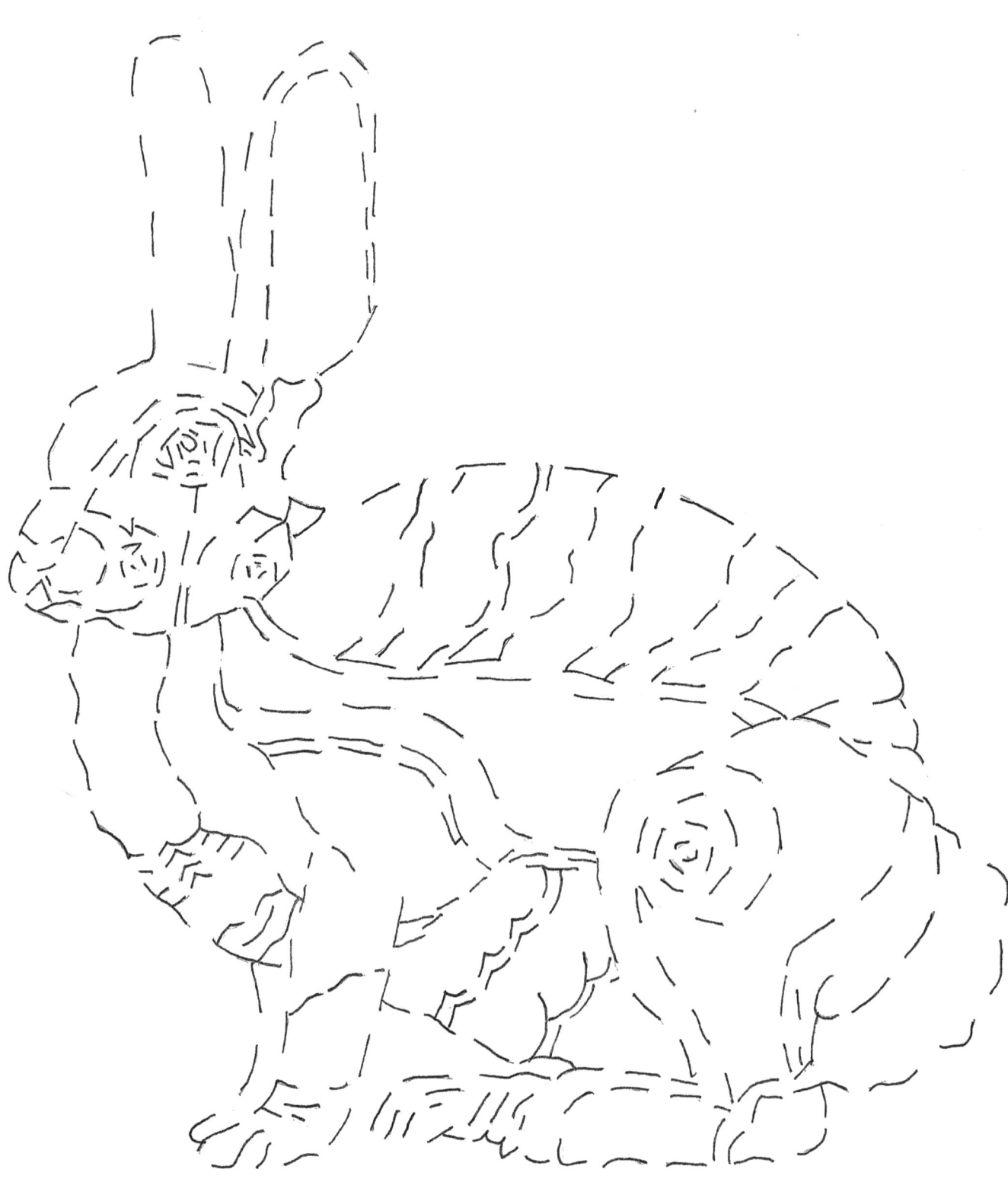

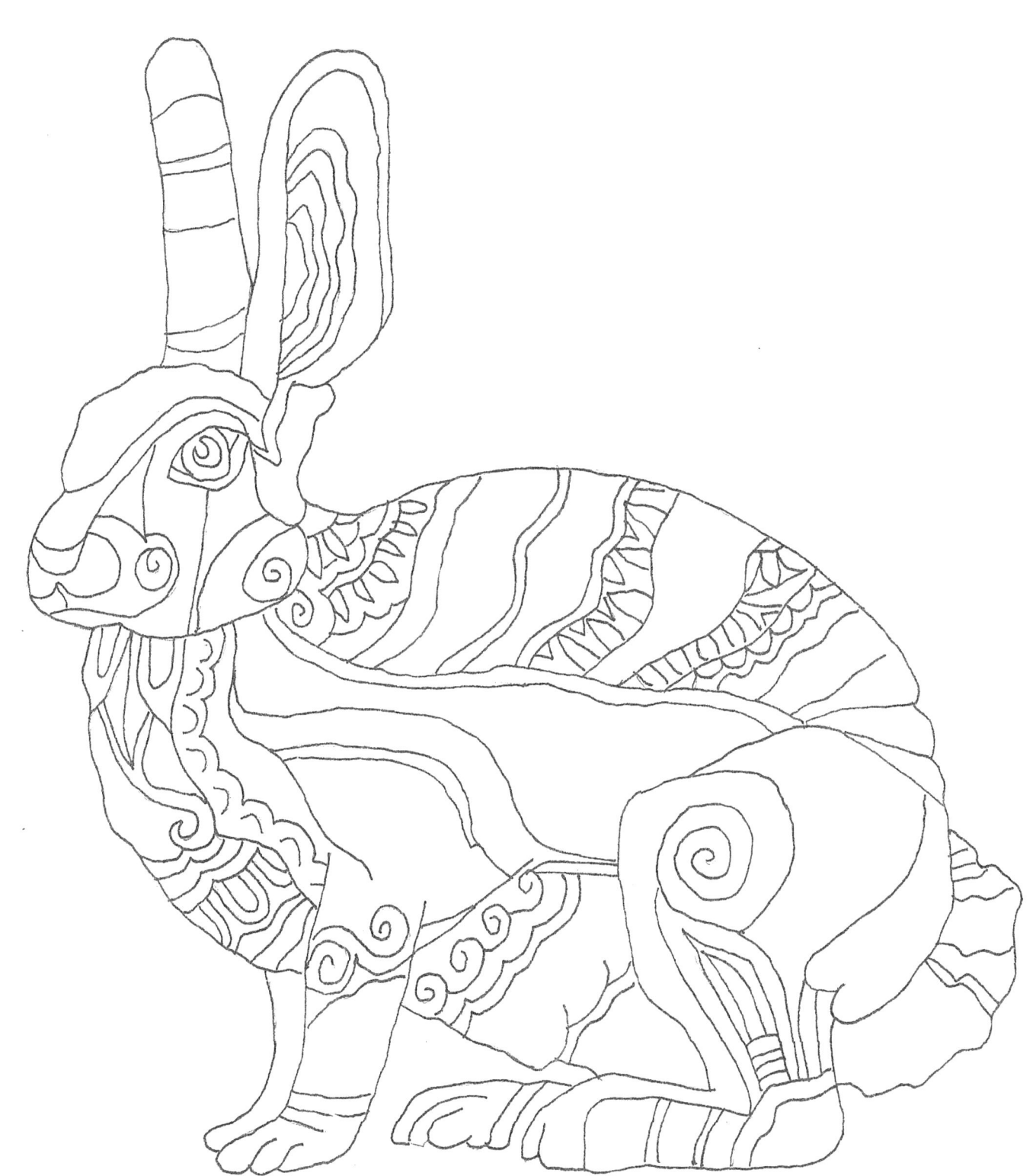

Do not reward yourself with too many treats – You are not a dog.

Unrealistic expectations are the root of all heartache.

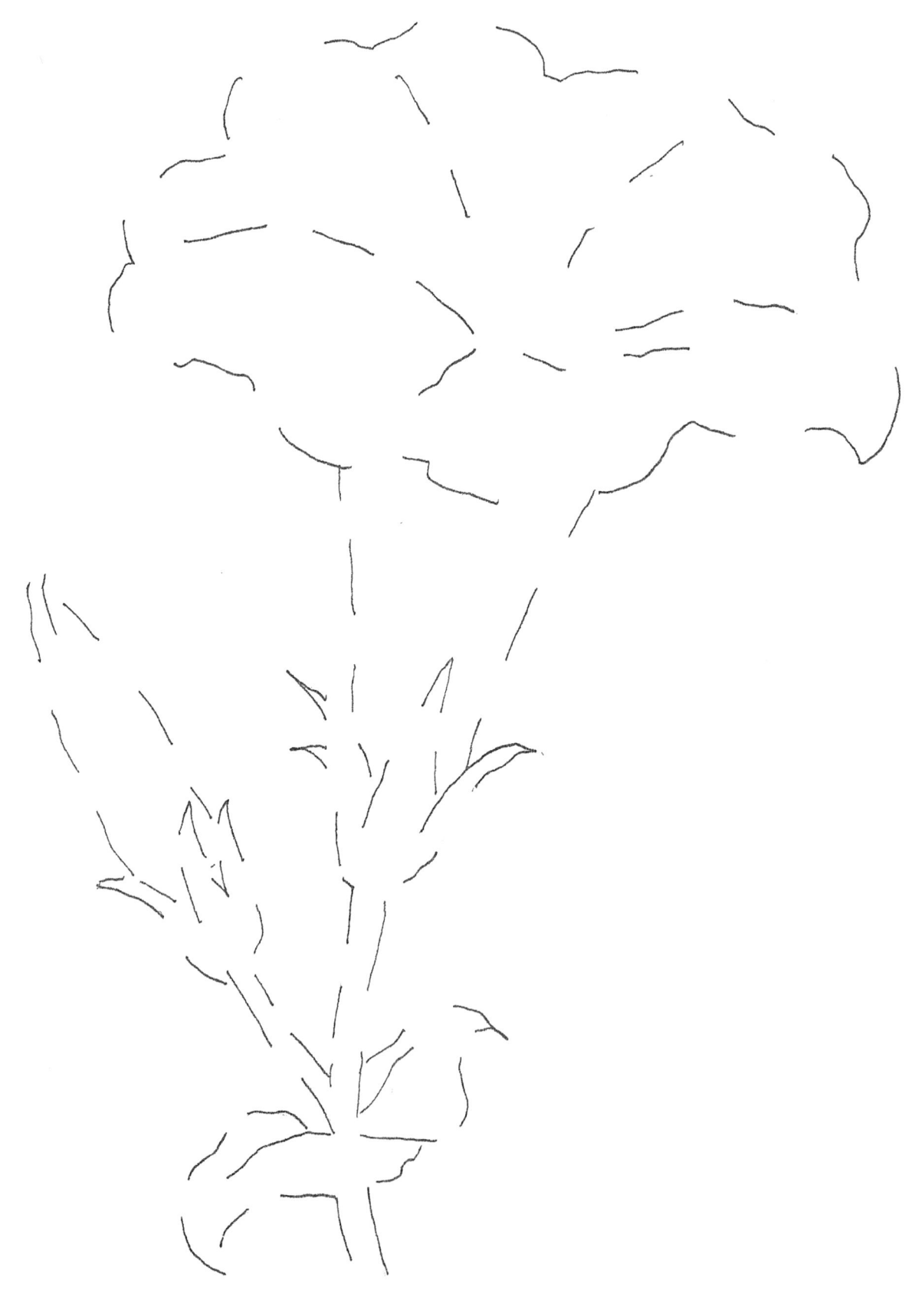

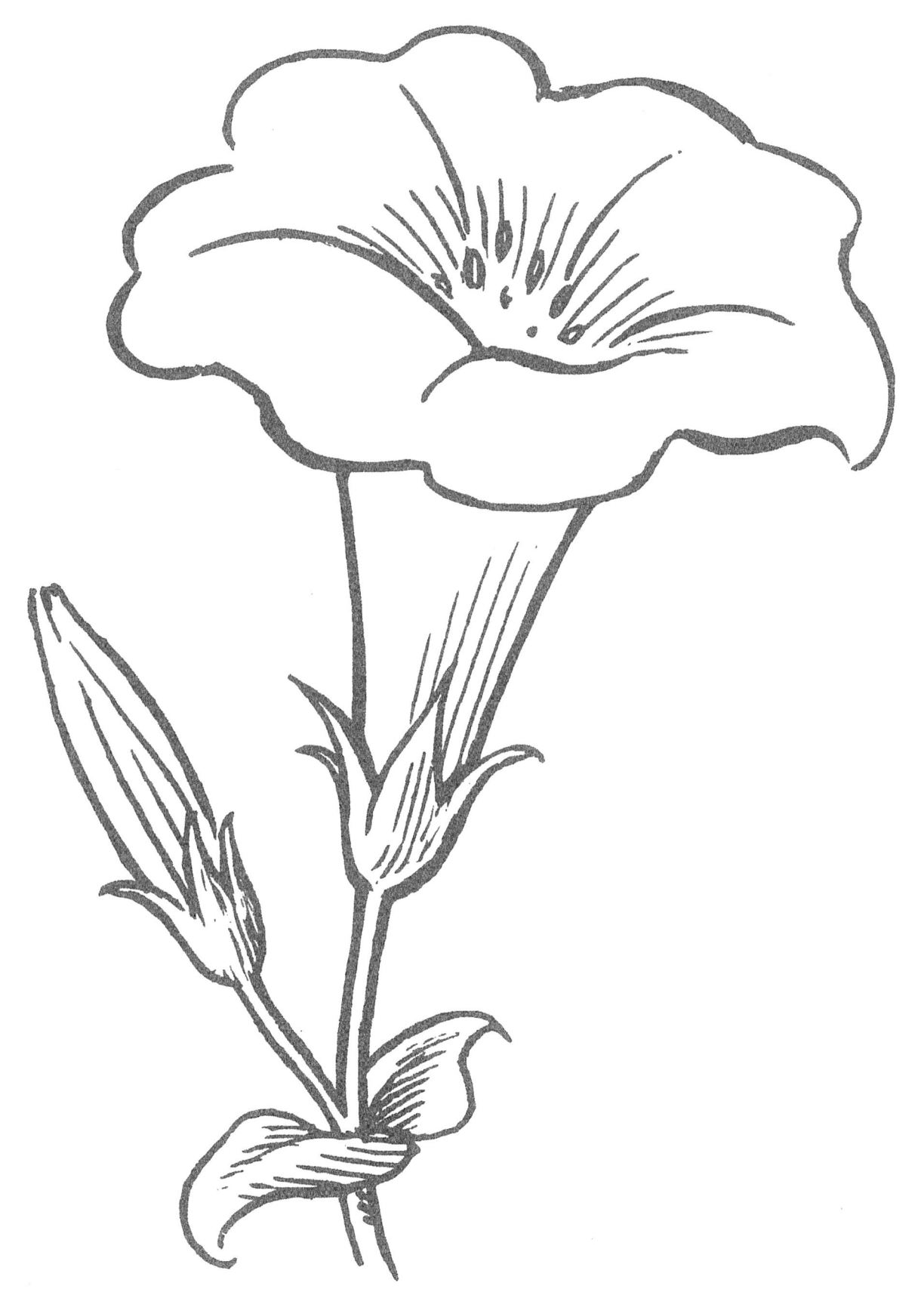

People usually see what they look for, and hear what they listen for.

To be inspired is great, but to inspire is an honor.

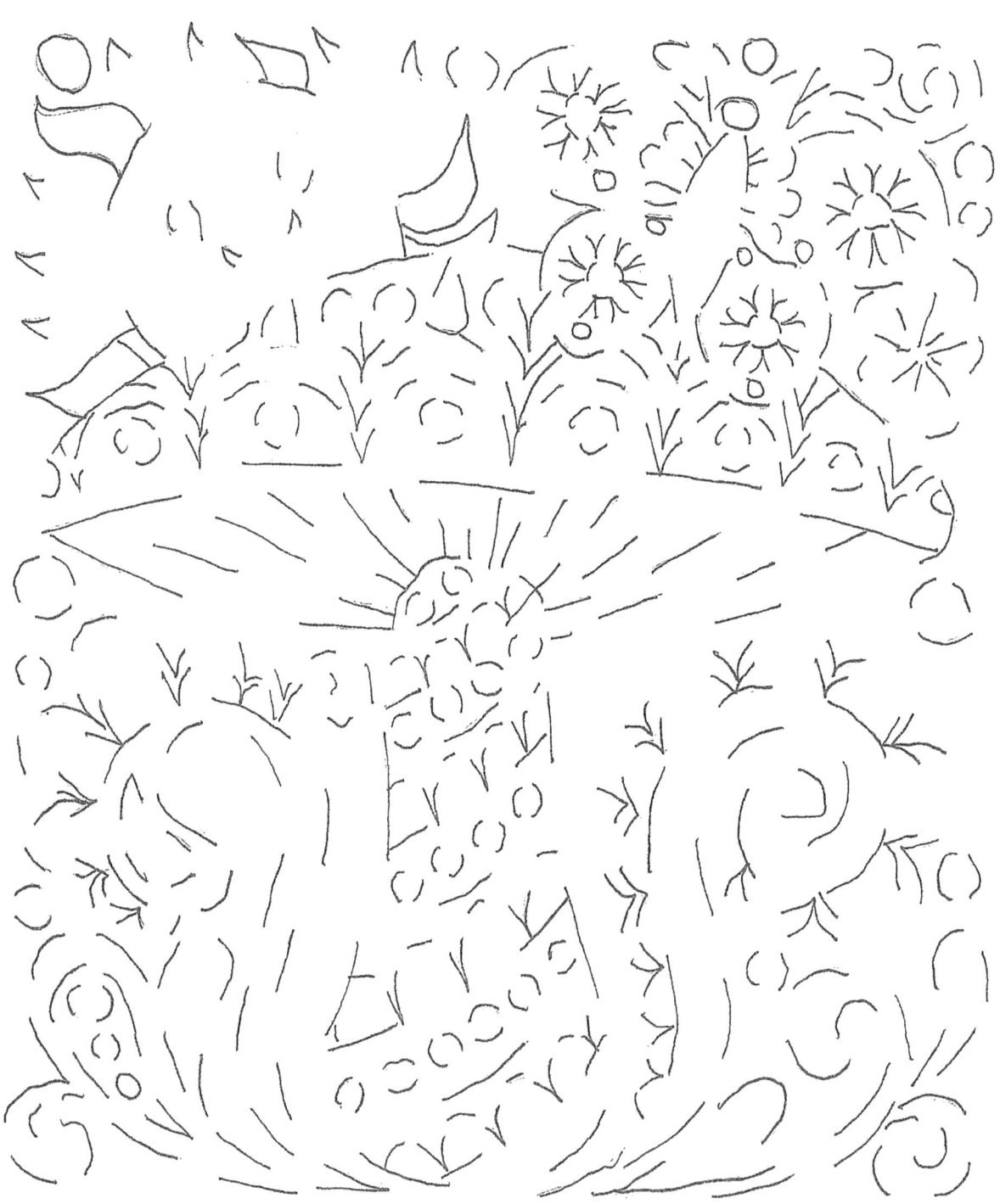

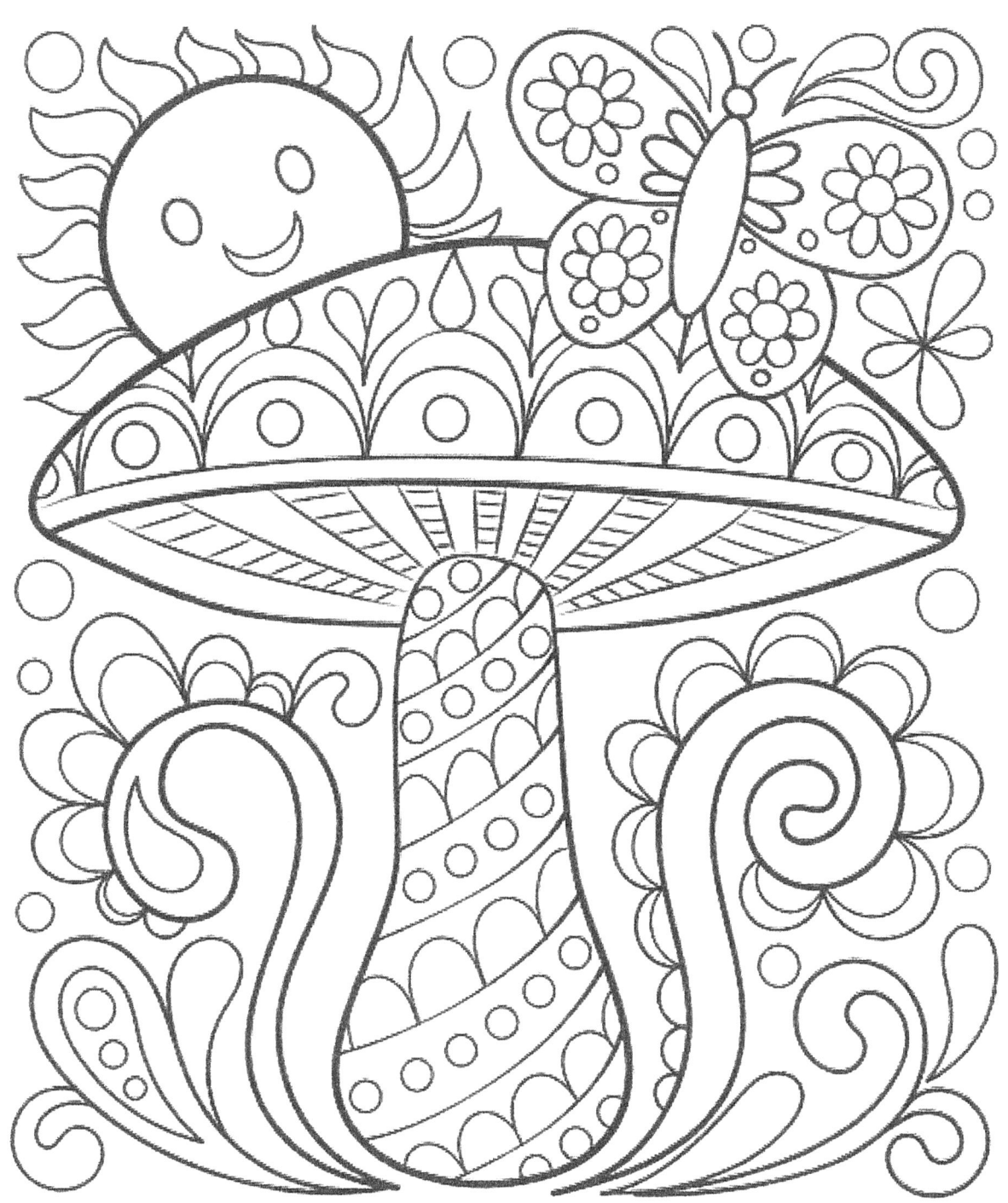

Don't be afraid to sit in the front row of your life.

We are all so desperate to be understood, we forget to be understanding.

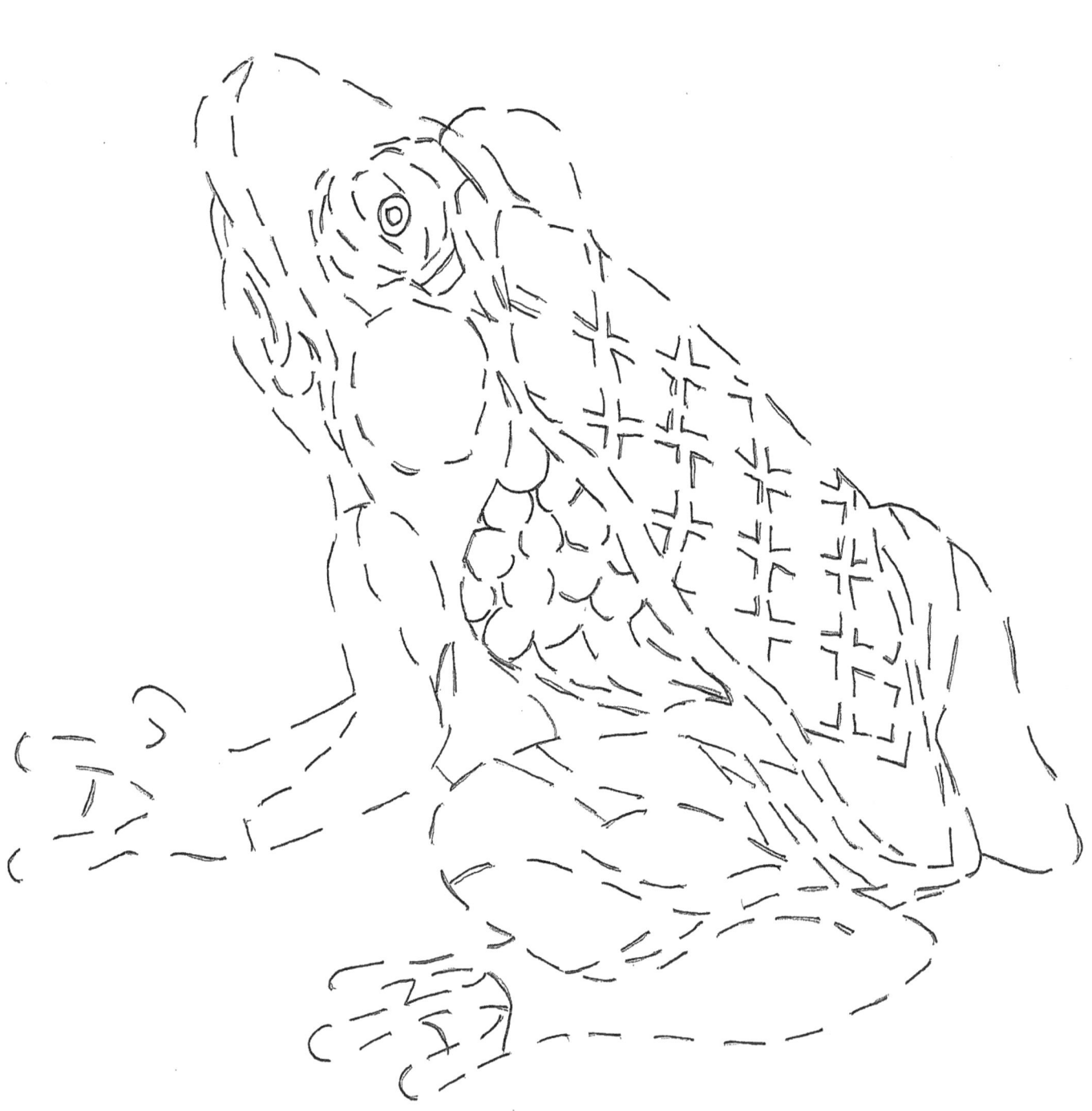

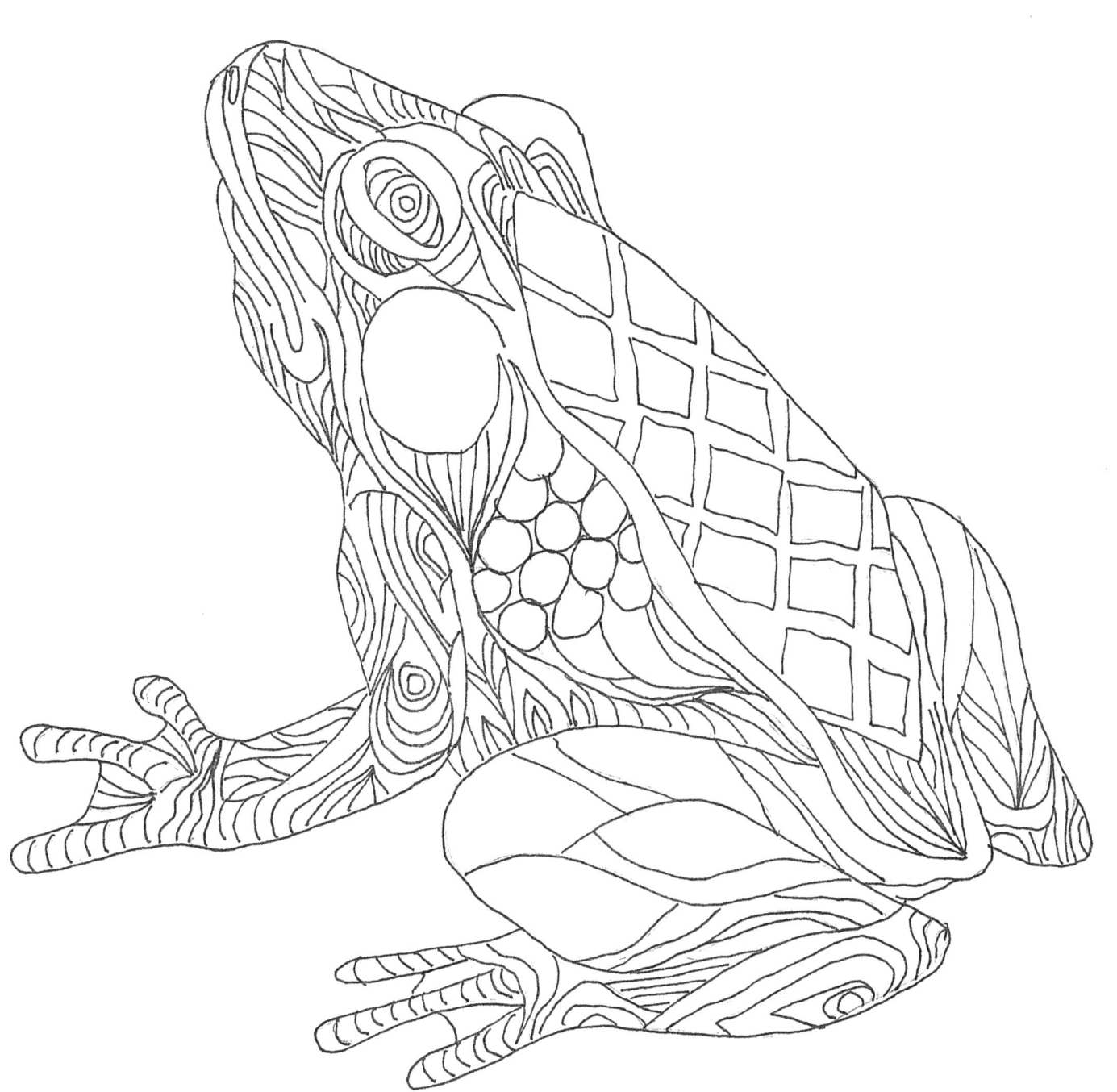

What we see depends mainly on what we look for.

It always seems impossible until it is done.

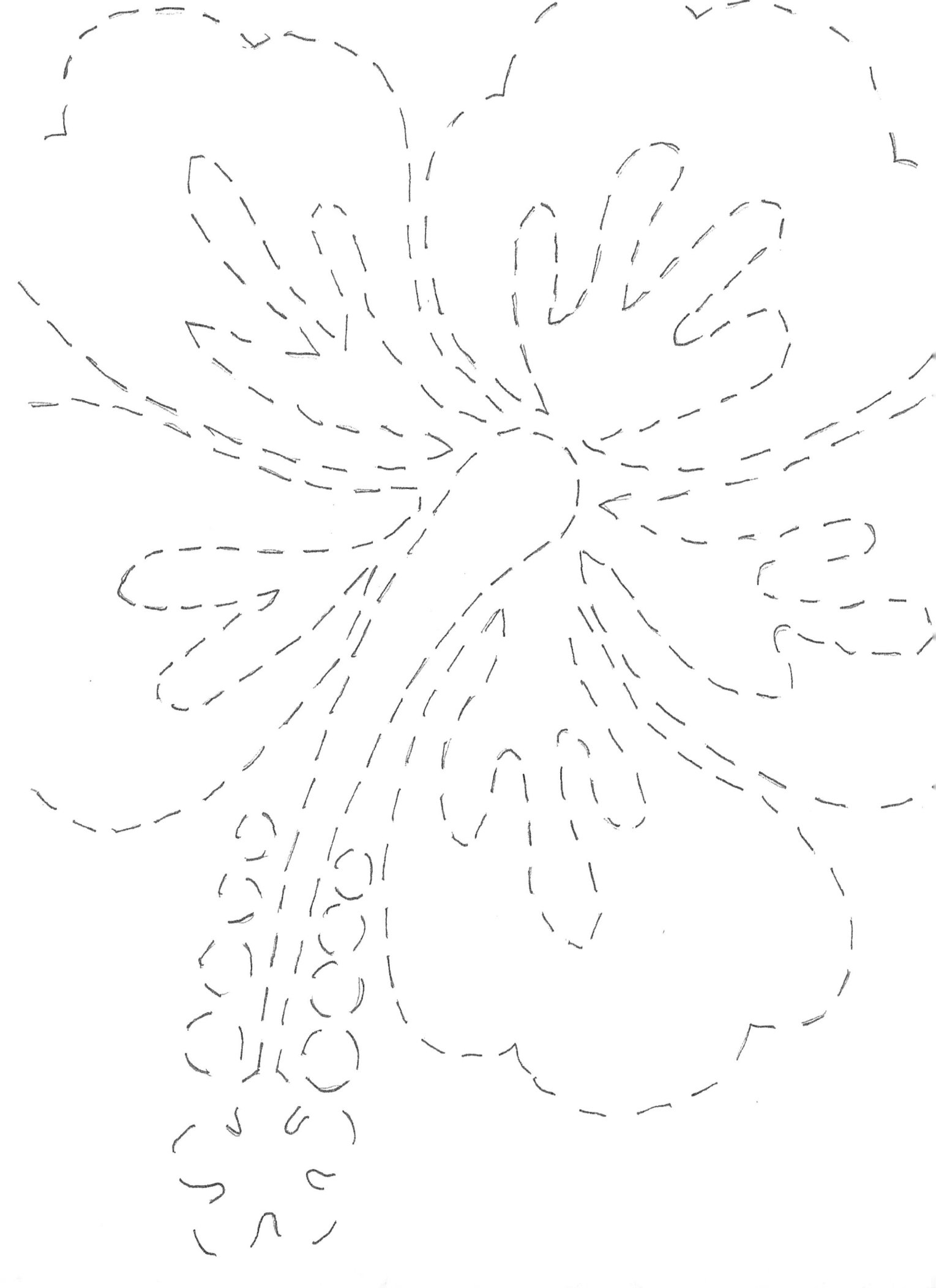

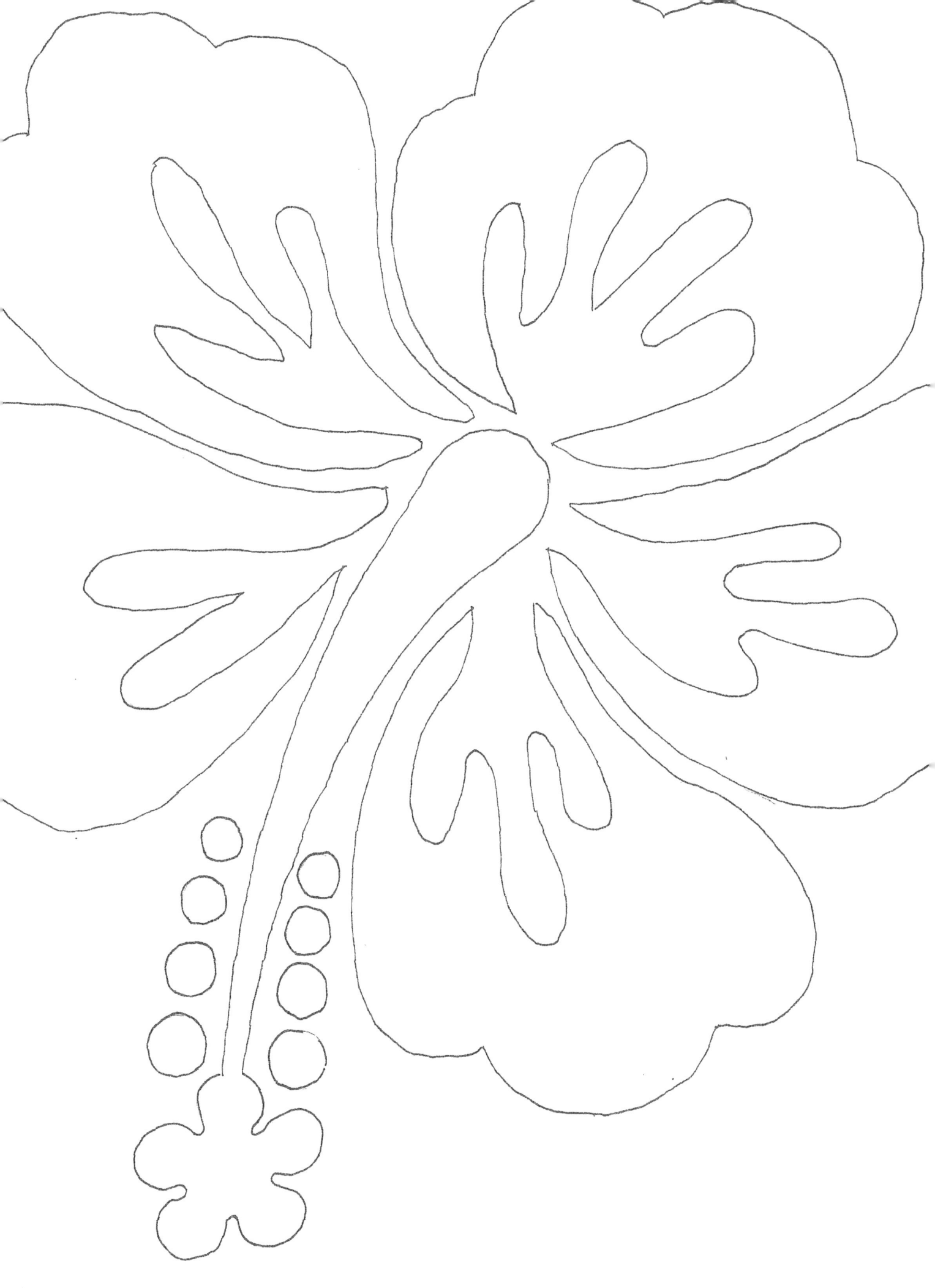

Be there for others but never leave yourself behind.

Loyalty is hard to find and Trust is easy to lose.

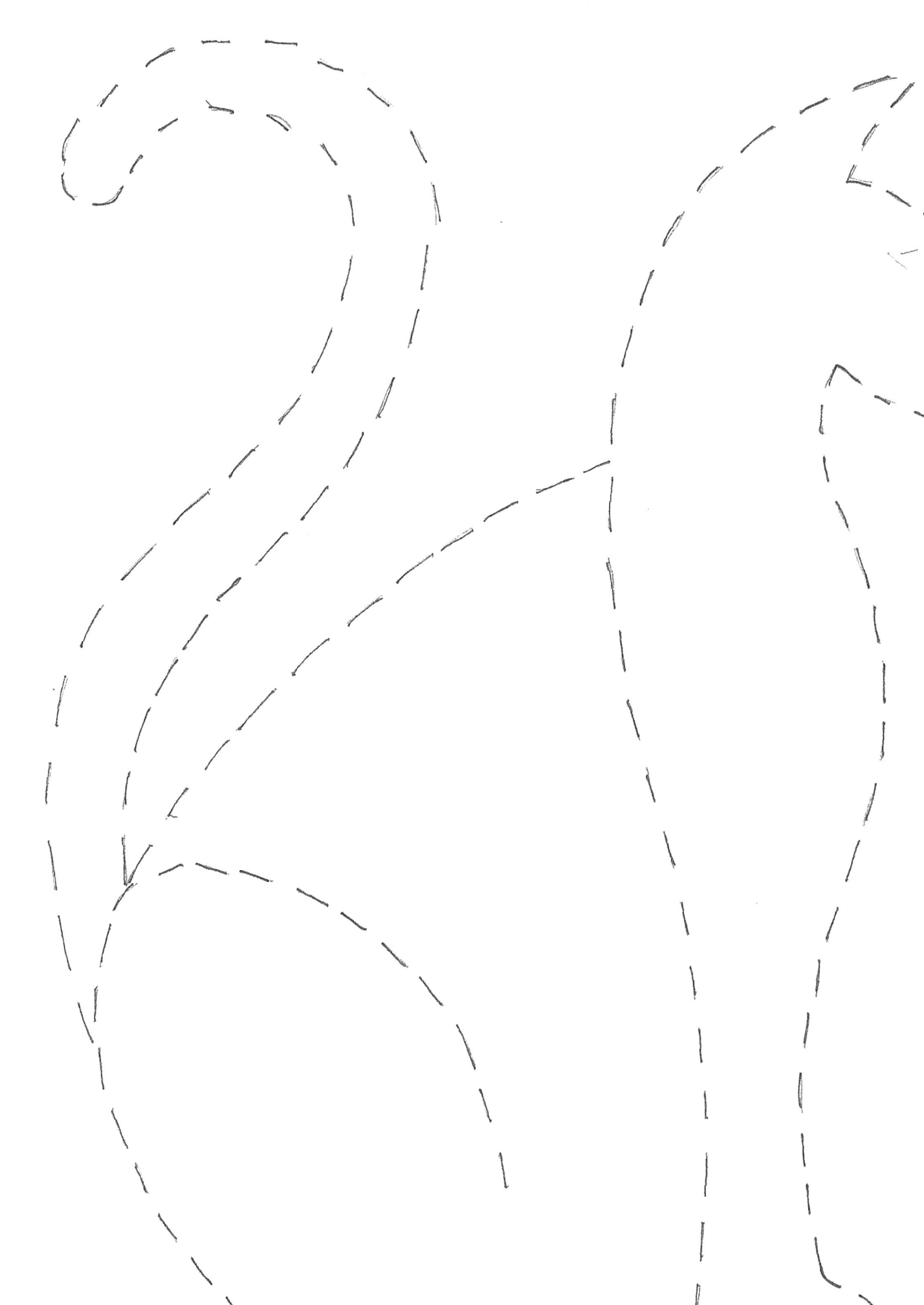

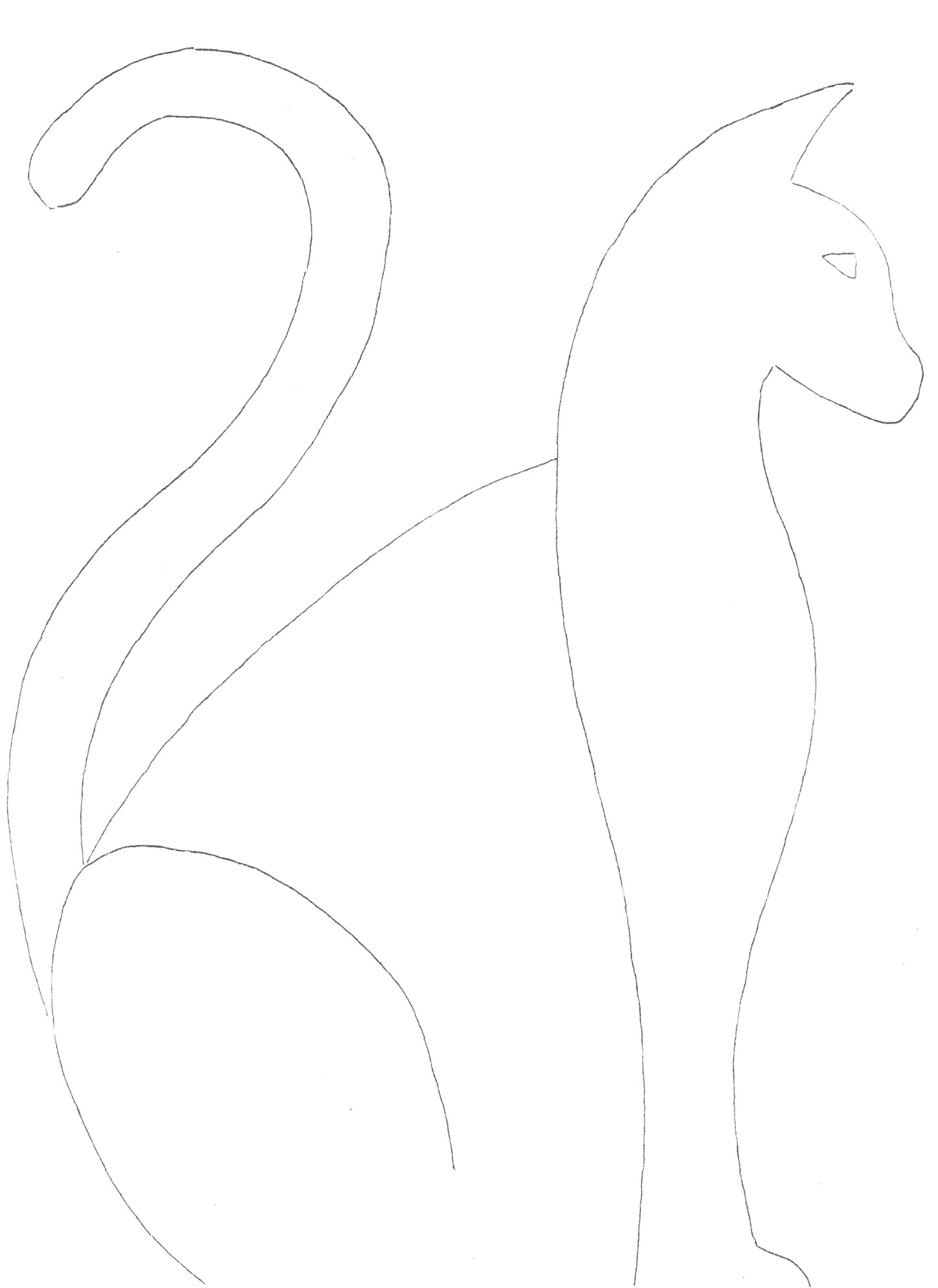

You can't pour from an empty cup.

Believing you can is half the battle.

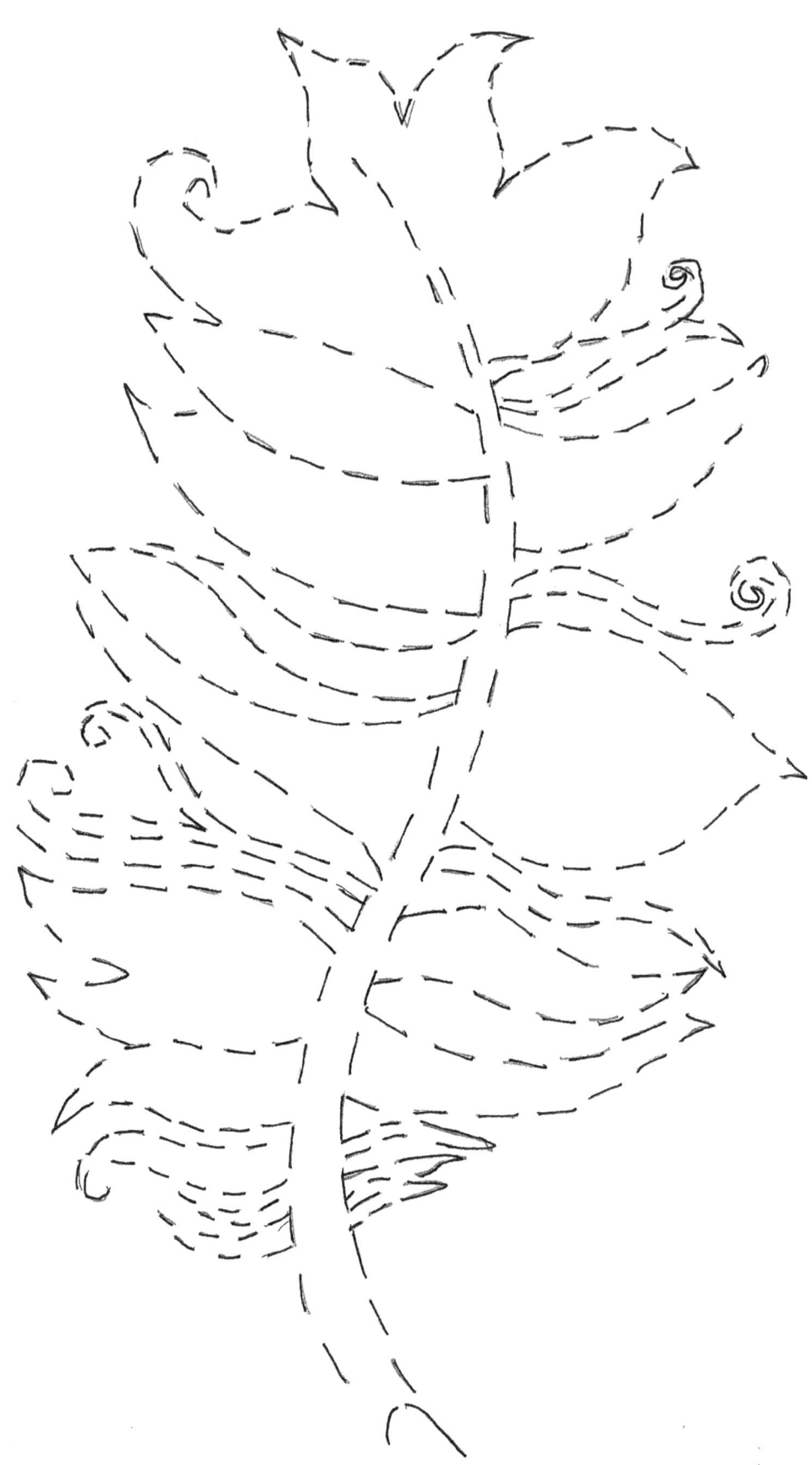

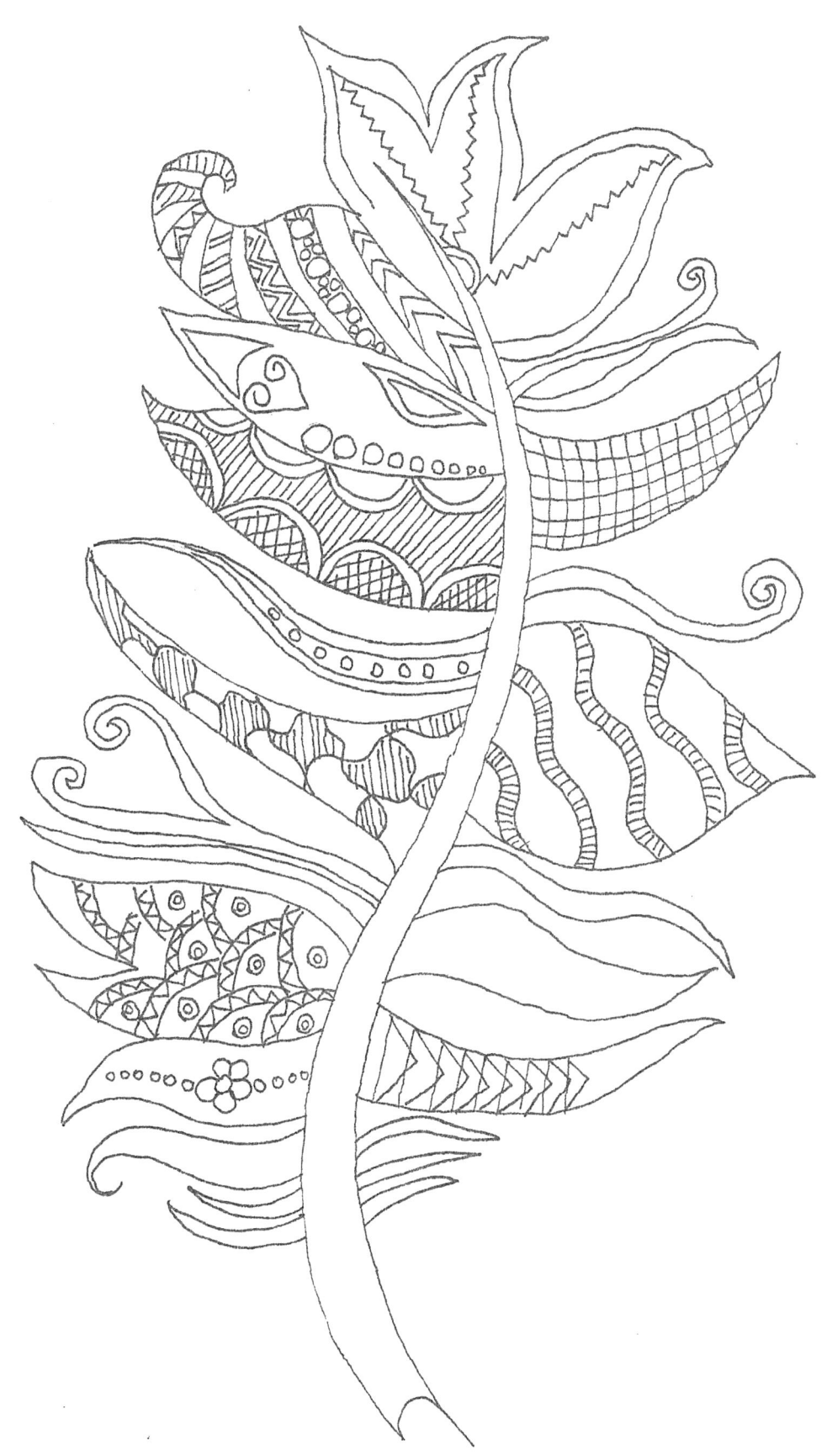

Do not force the development of mindfulness.

One who is patient glows with an inner radiancy.

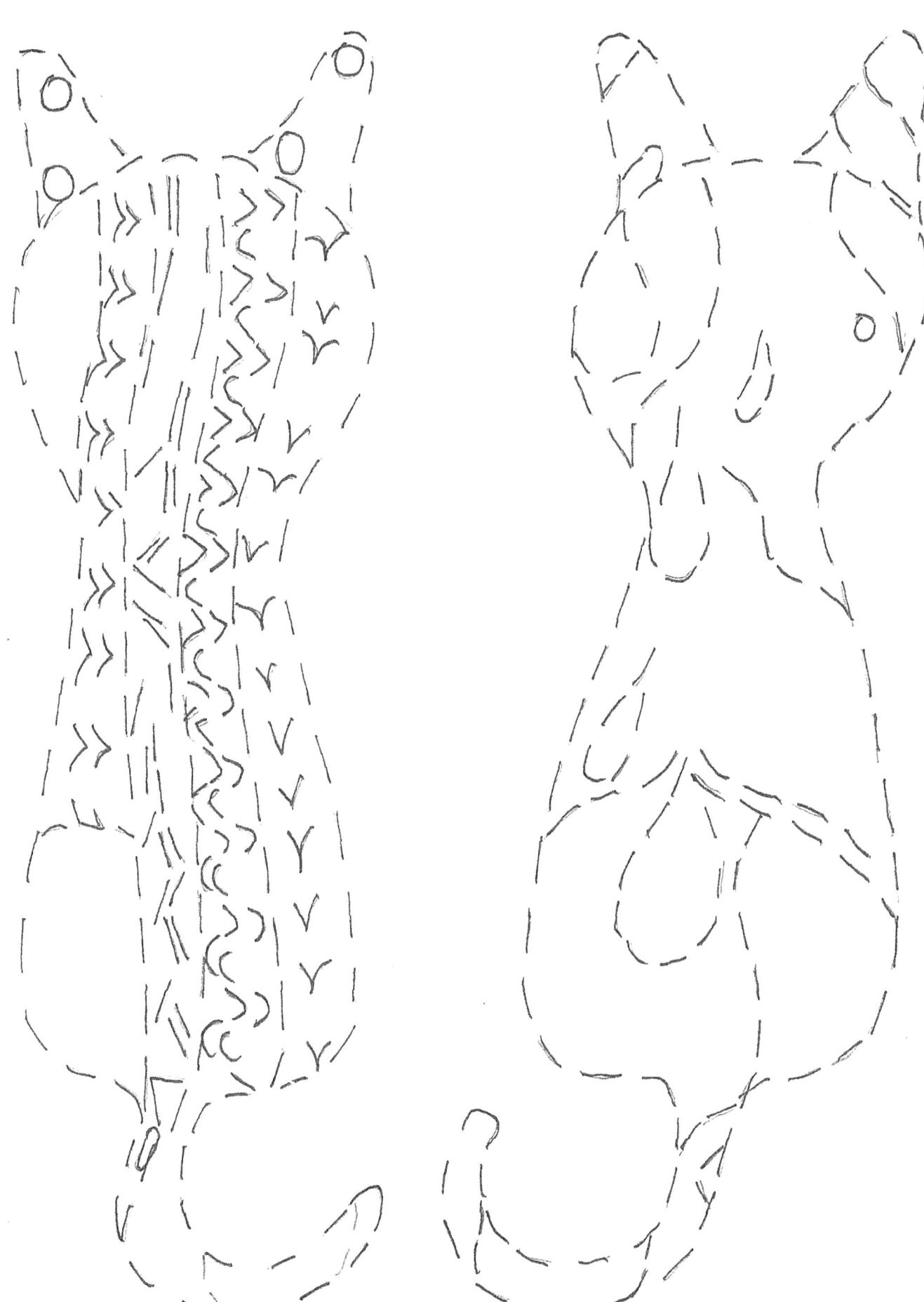

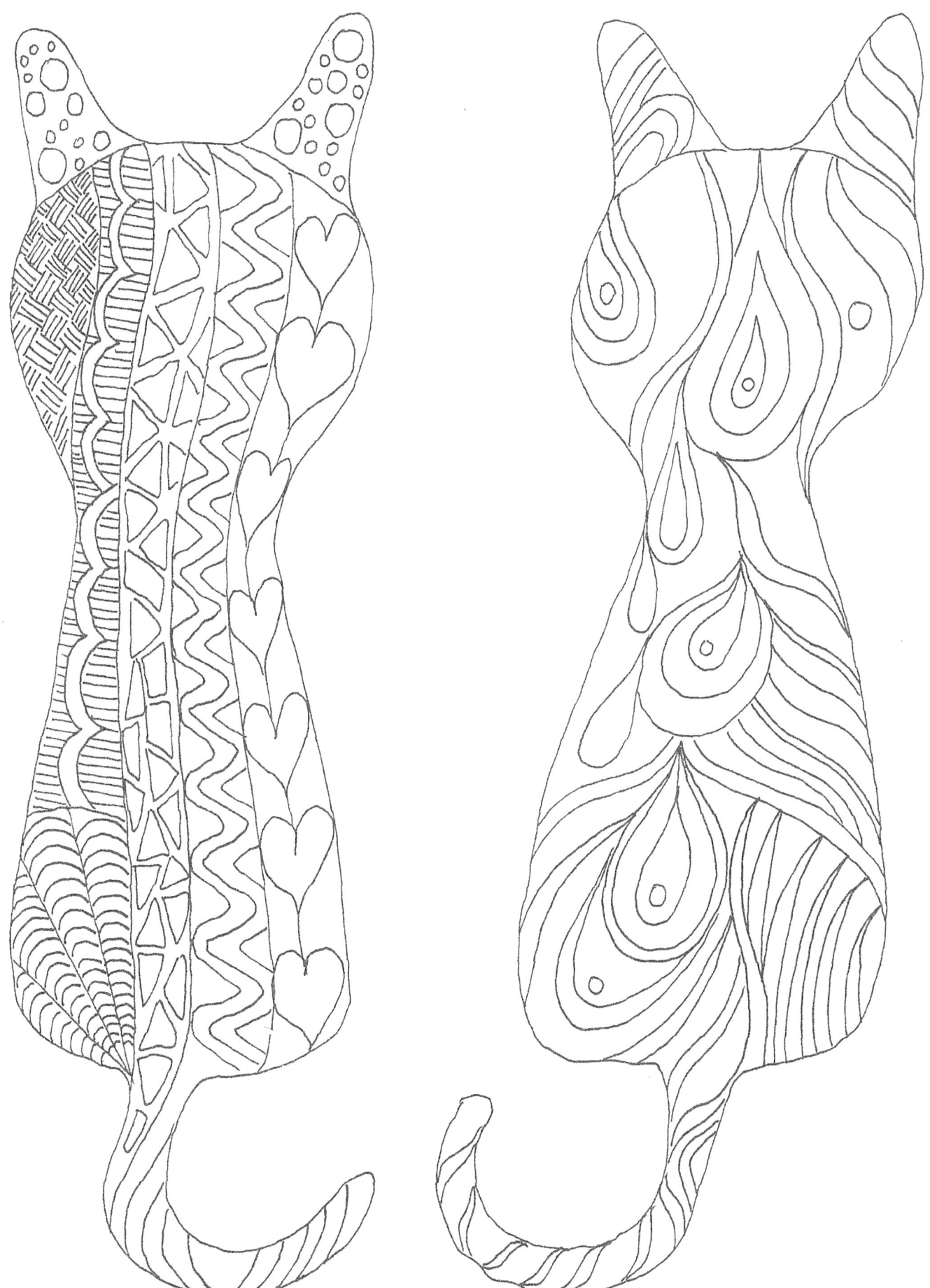

Patience is both the tool for and the result of, out efforts.

Compassion is not complete if it does not include oneself.

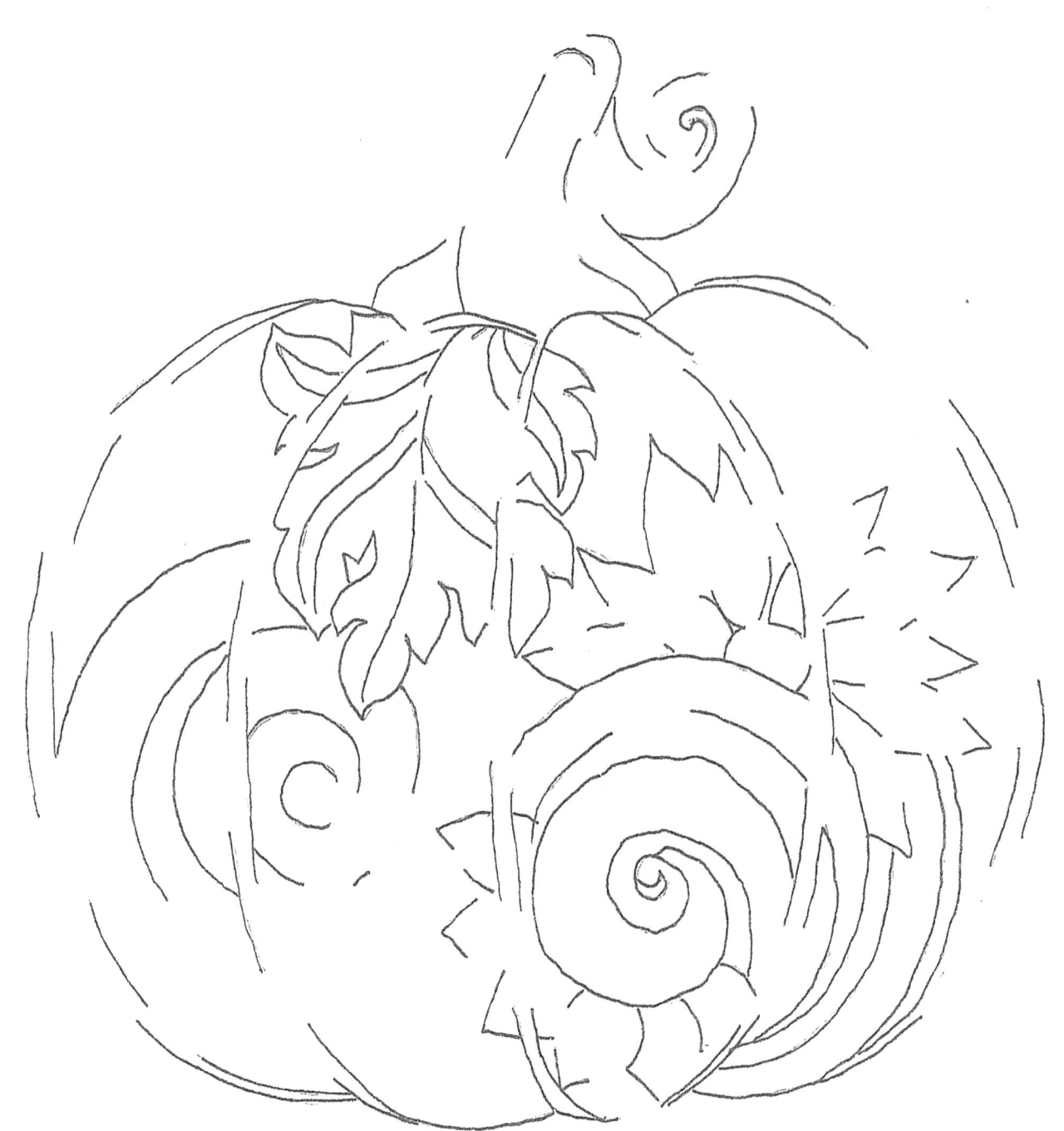

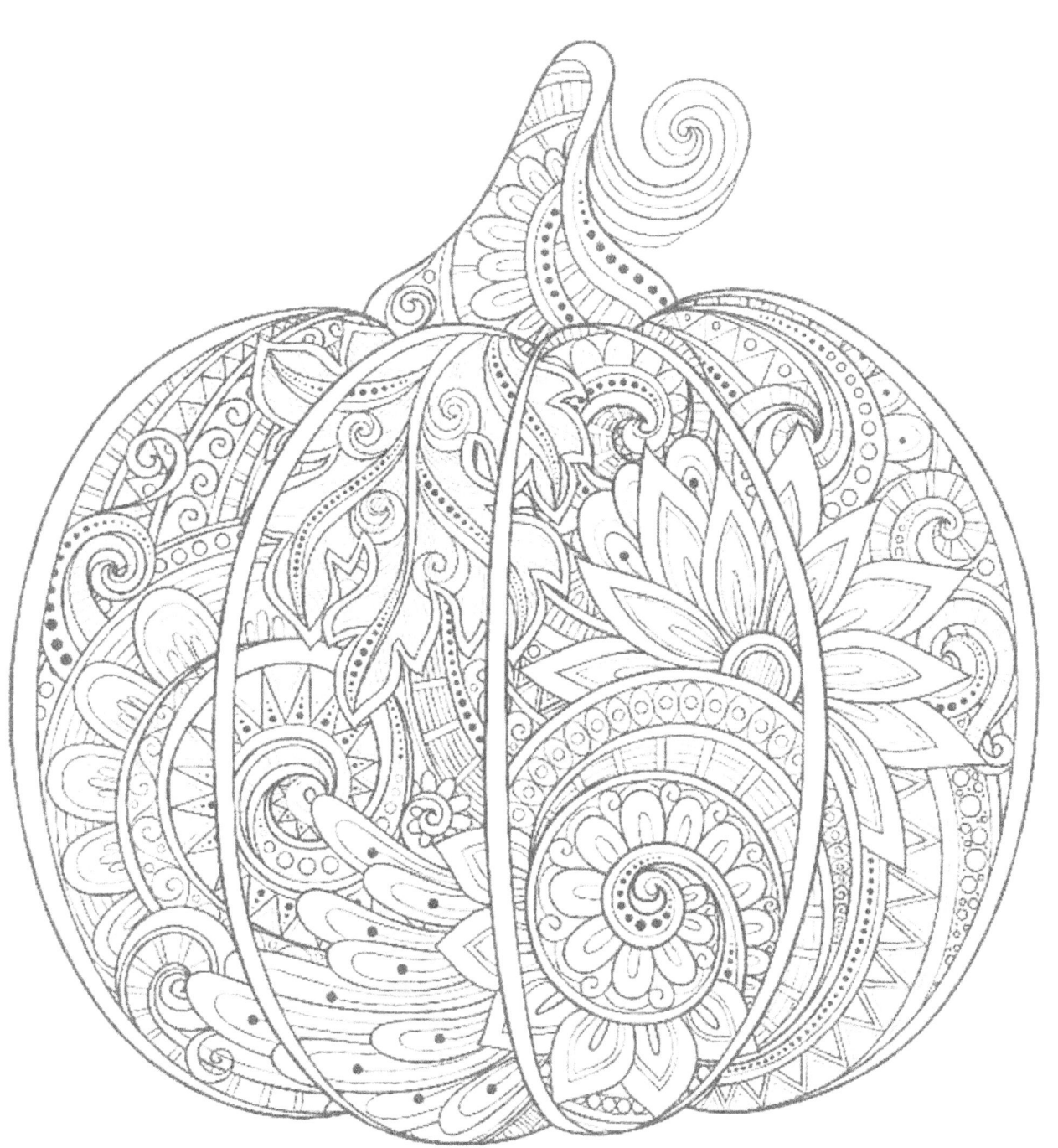

Each place is the right place—the place where I now am can be sacred.

Your actions are your only true belongings.

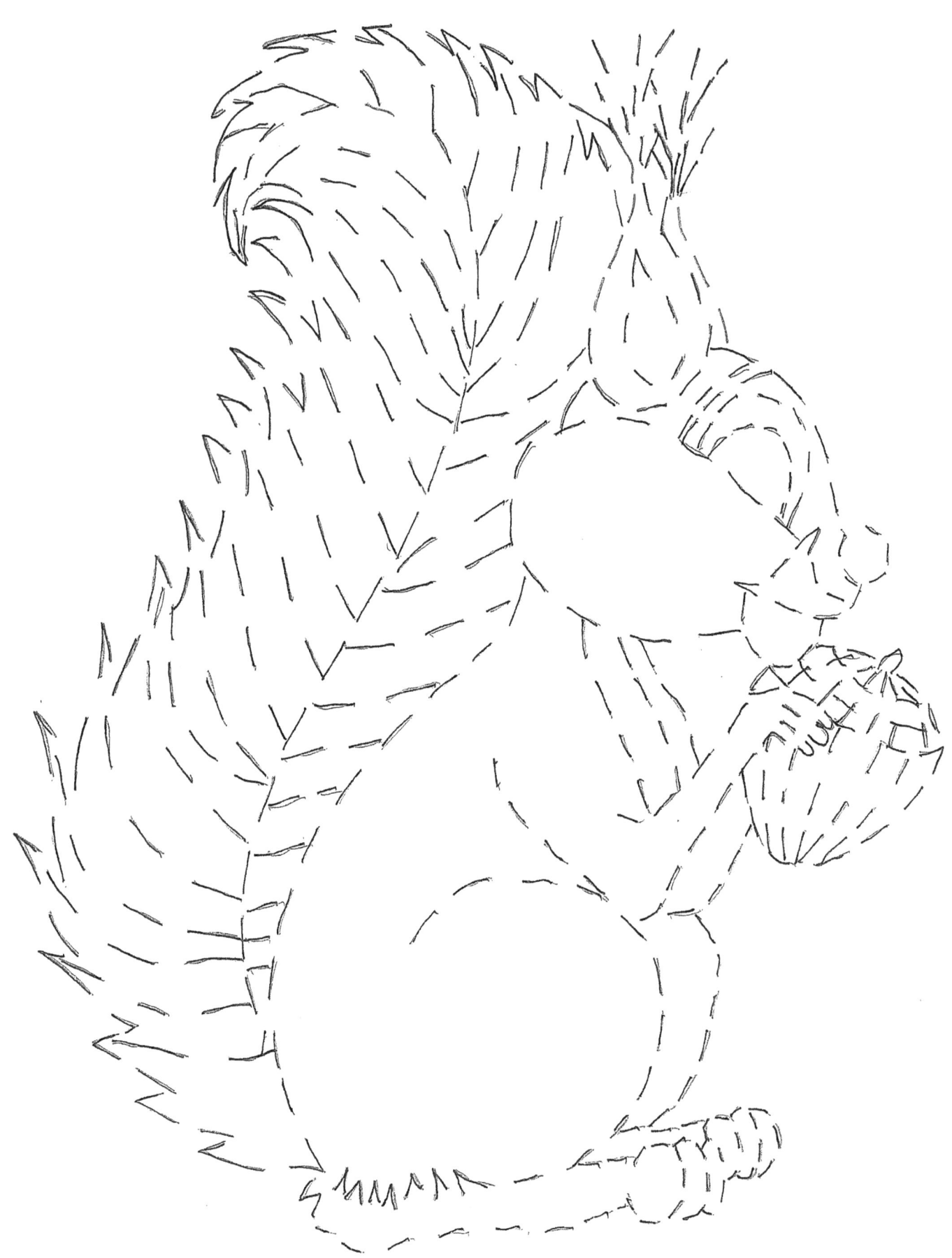

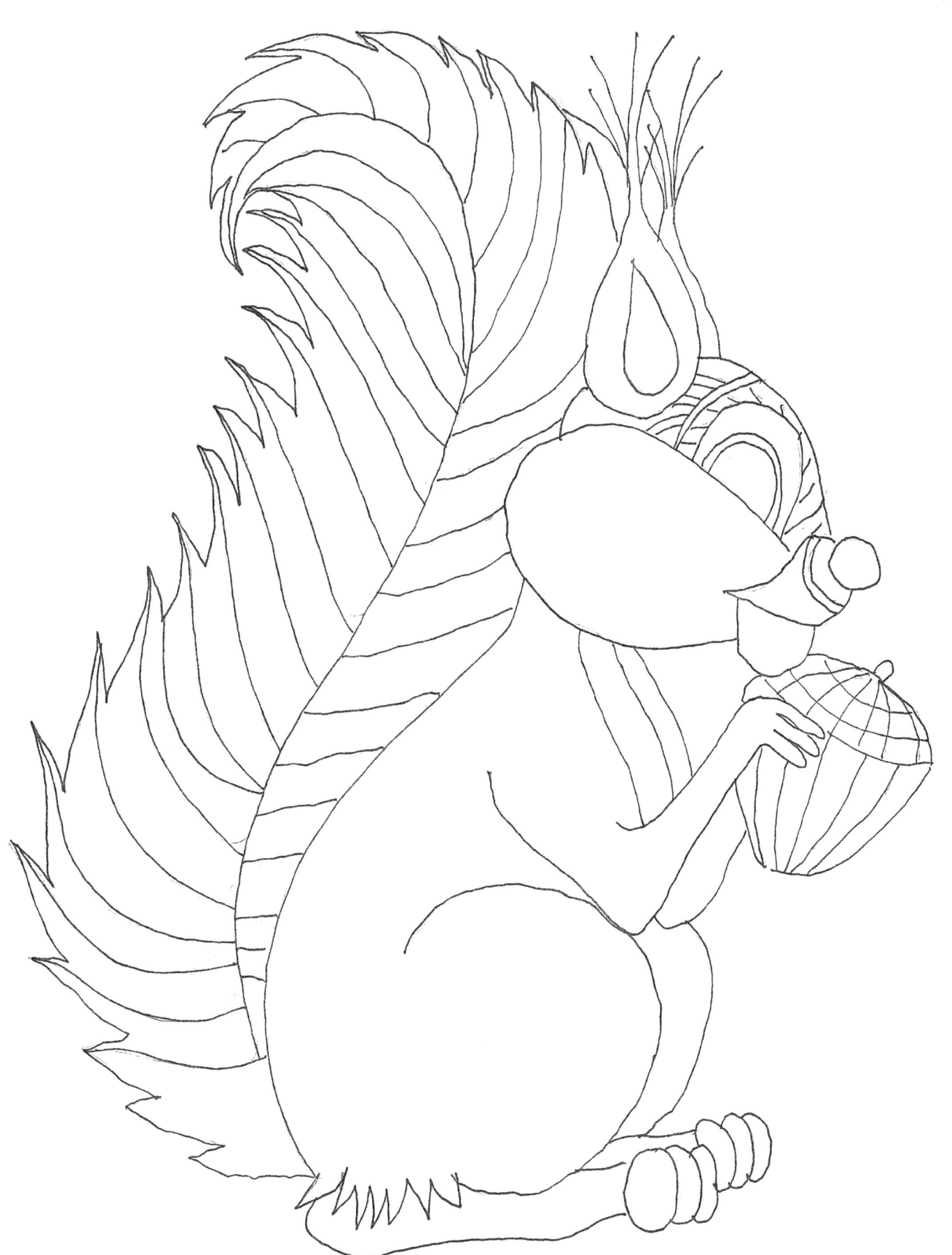

Patience has all the time it needs.

It's good to have a end in mind but the end that counts is how you travel.

It's good to have a end in mind but the end that counts is how you travel.

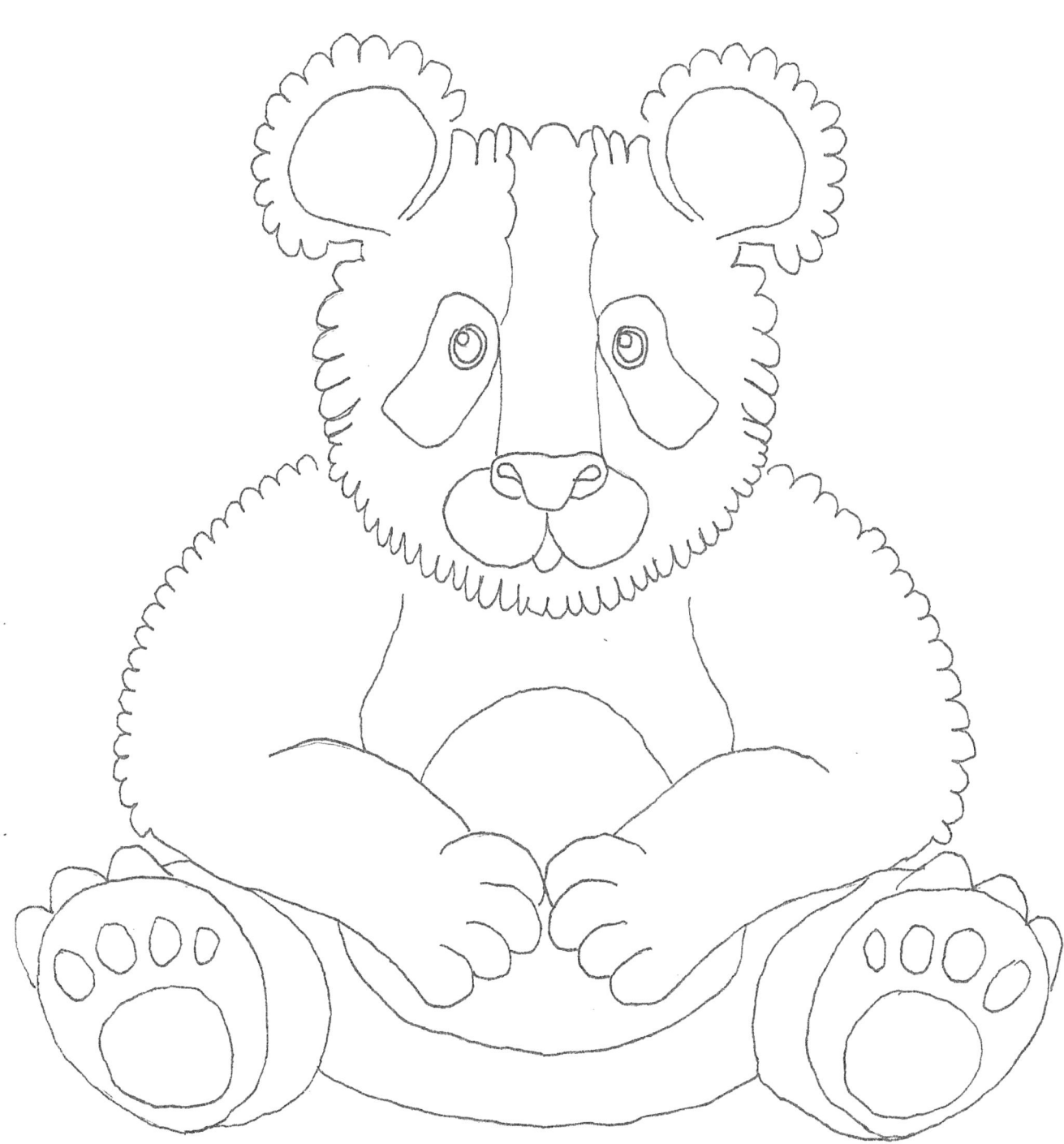

Treat everyone you meet as if they were you.

Meditation is the ultimate mobile device; you can use it anywhere, anytime, unobtrusively.

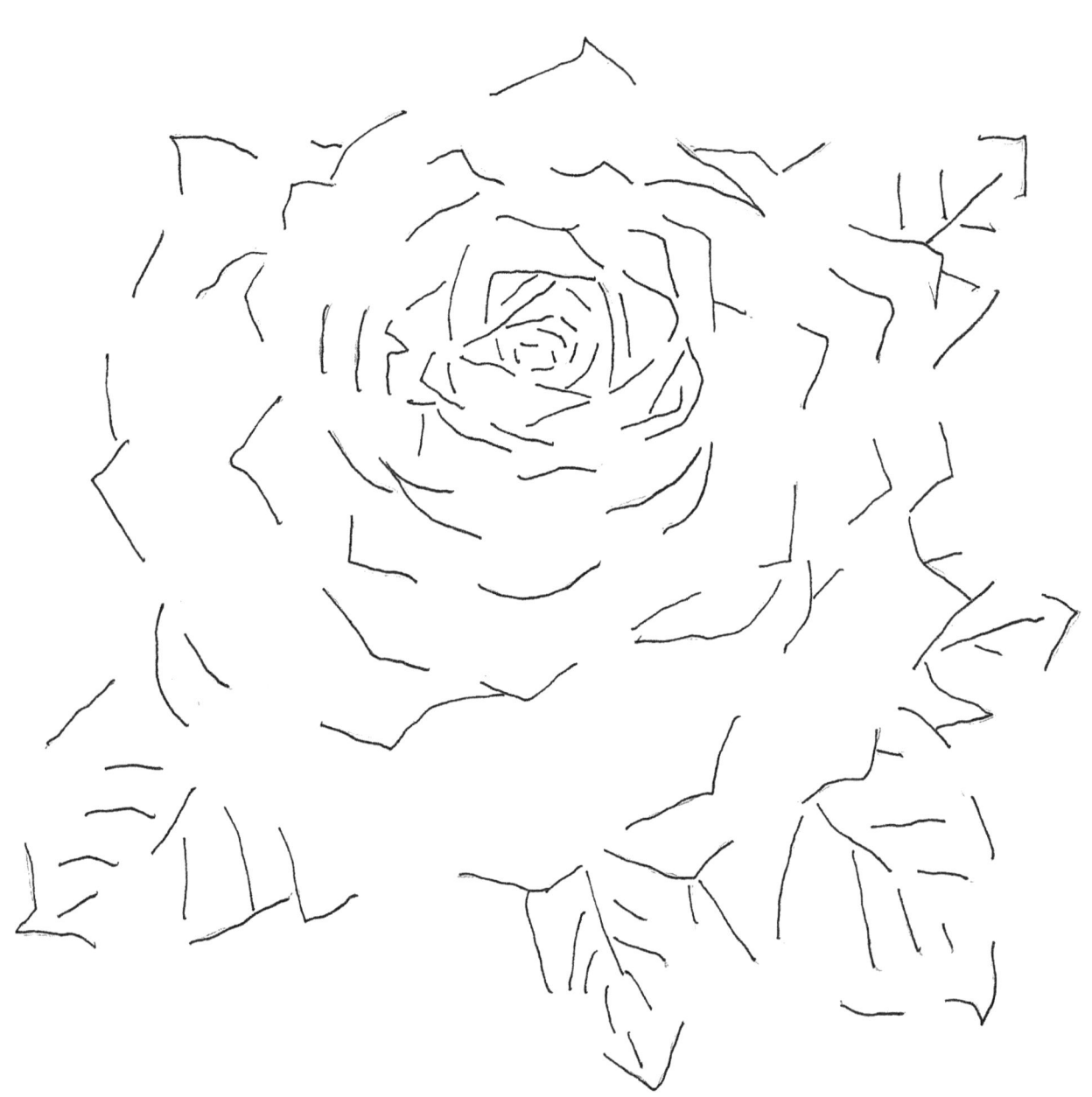

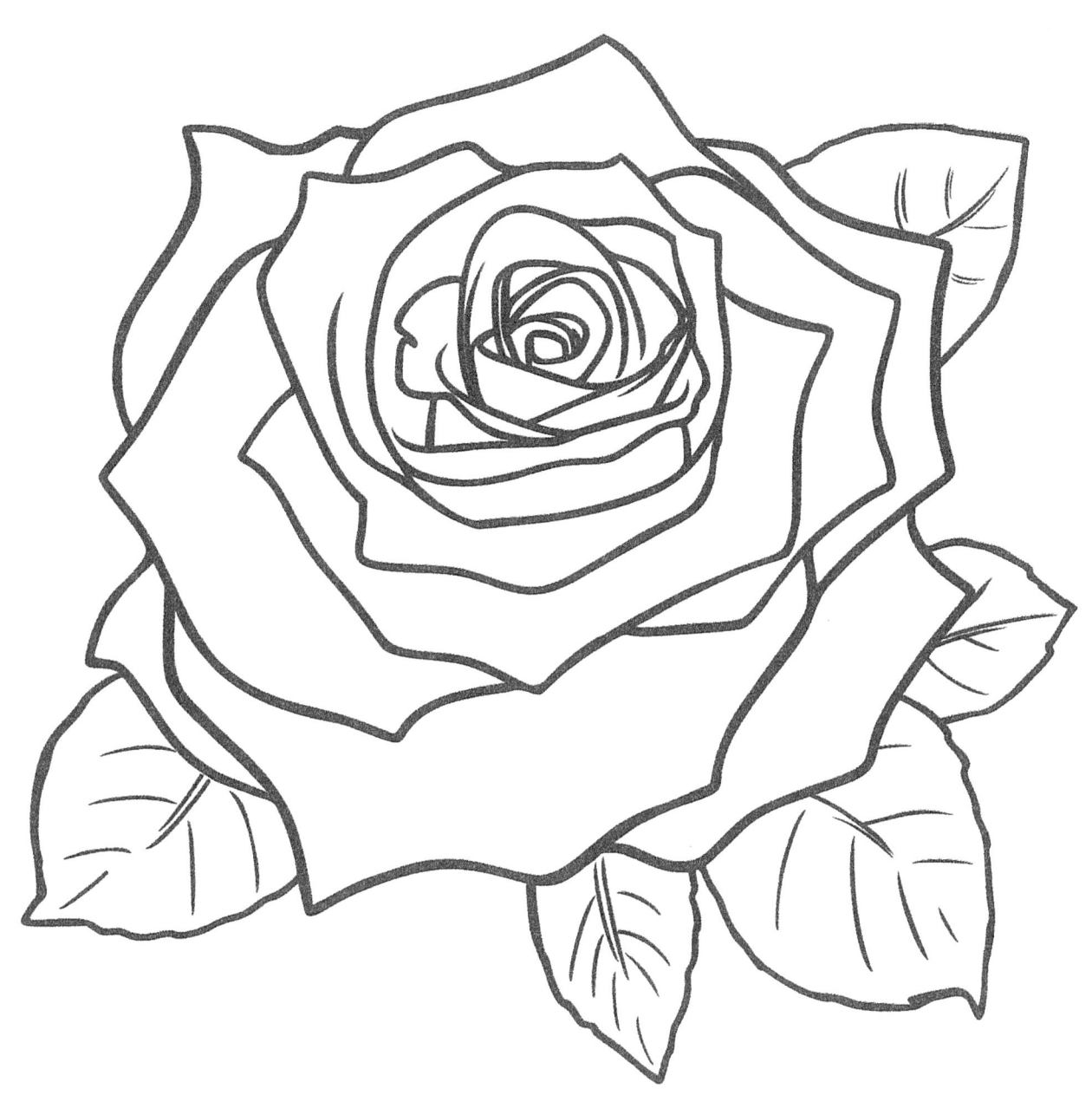

Life is a dance. Mindfulness is witnessing that dance.

Mindfulness isn't difficult; we just need to remember to do it.

Mindfulness isn't difficult; we just need to remember to do it.

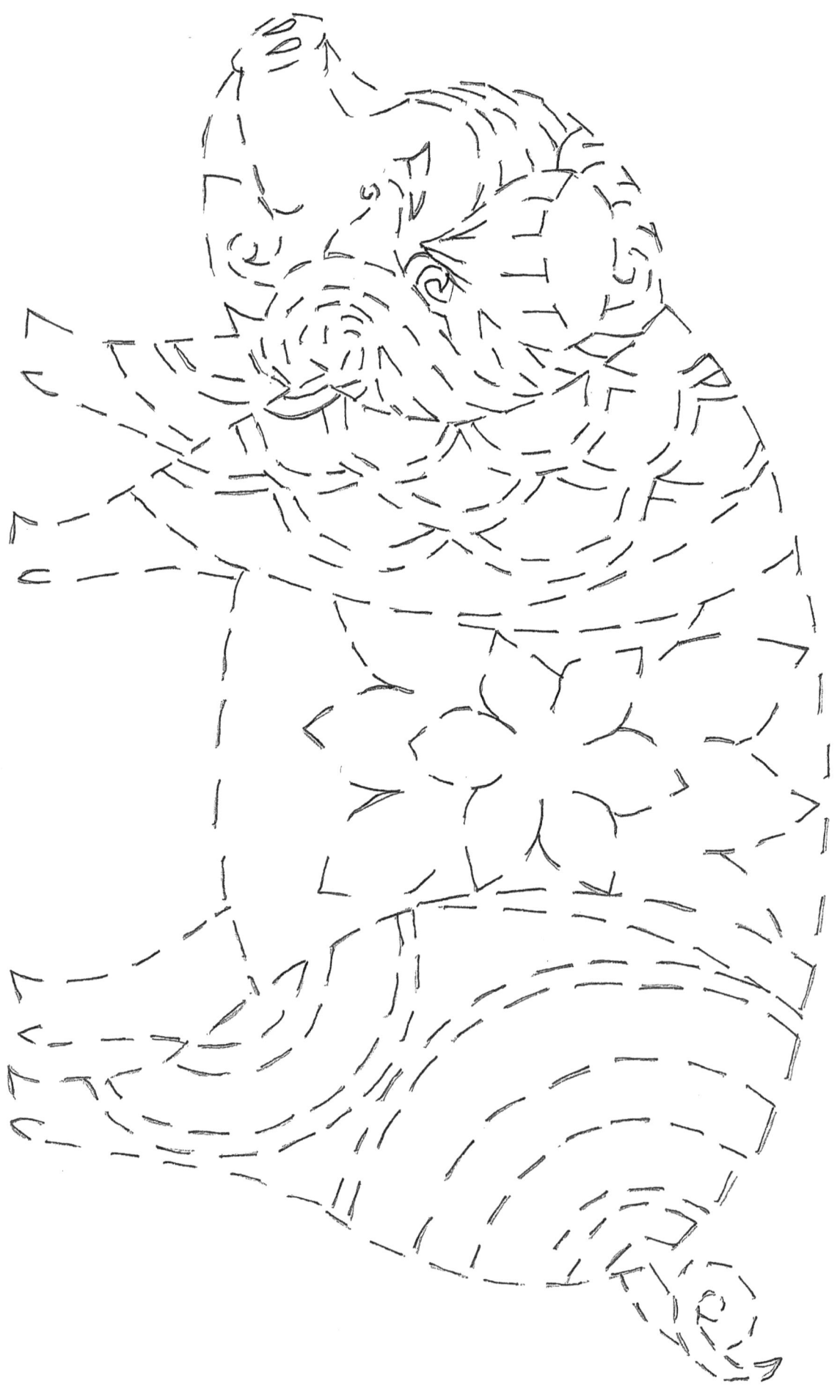

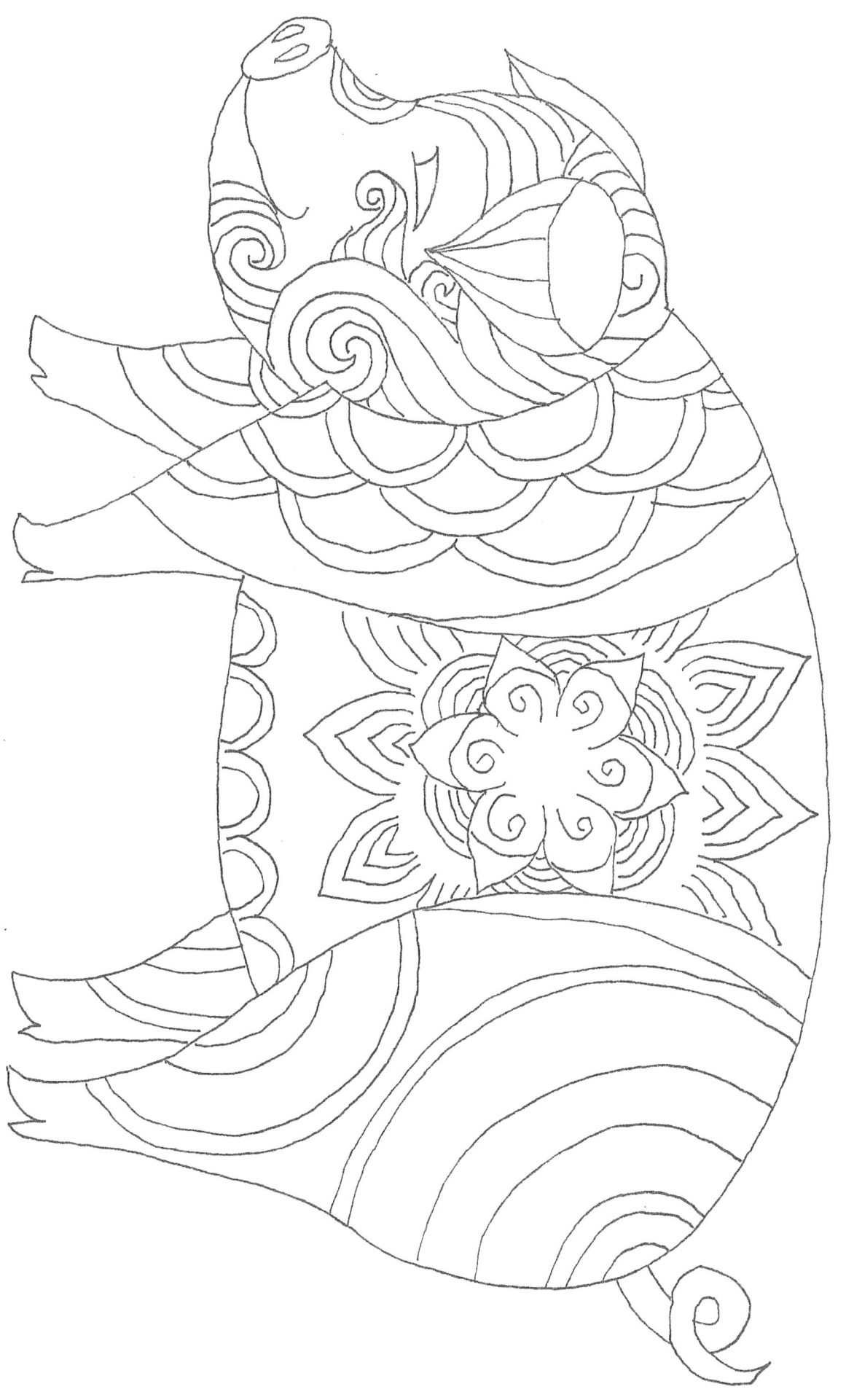

Envy and jealously stem from the fundamental inability to rejoice at someone else's happiness or success.

Begin at once to live, and count each separate day as a separate life.

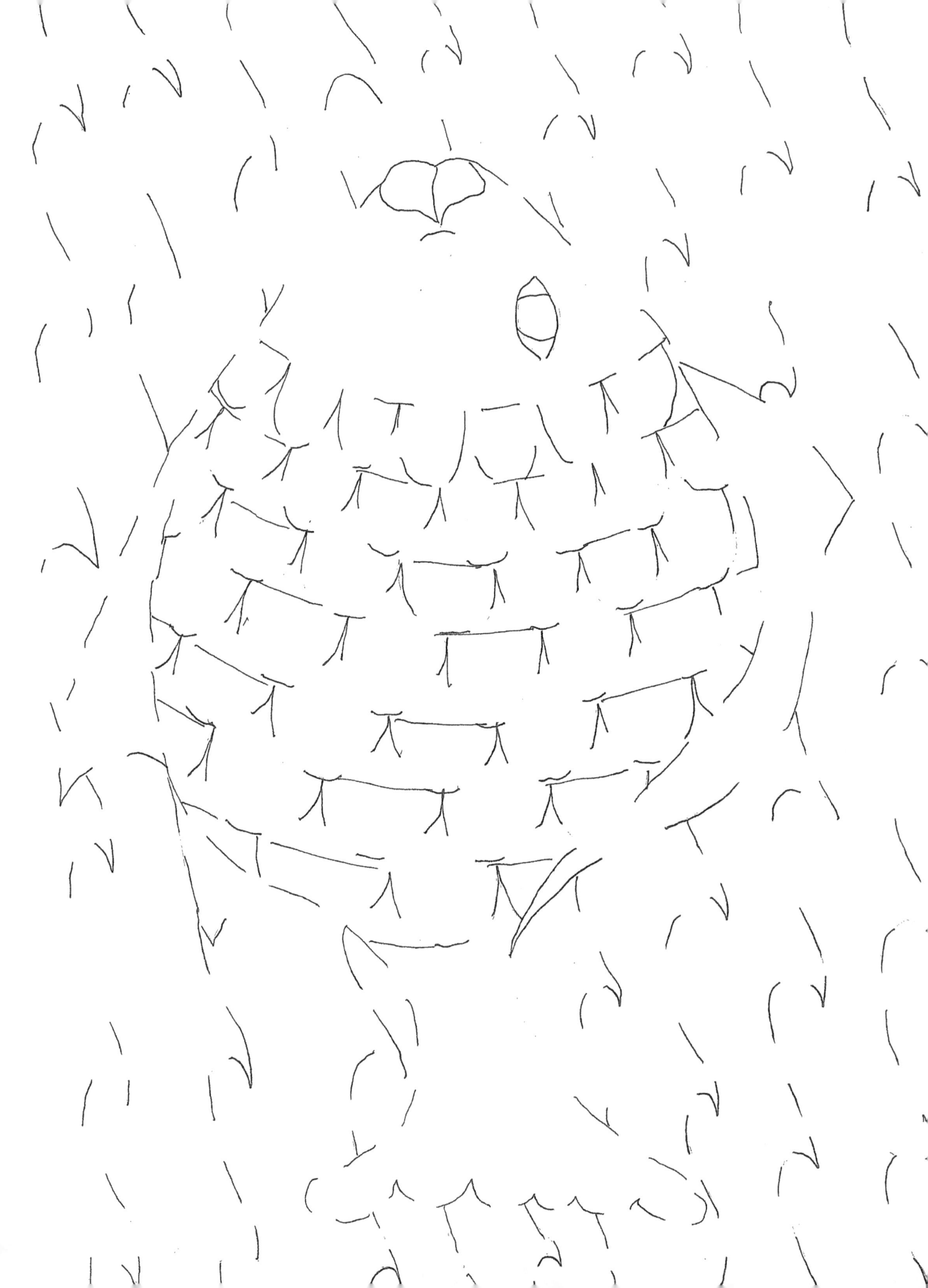

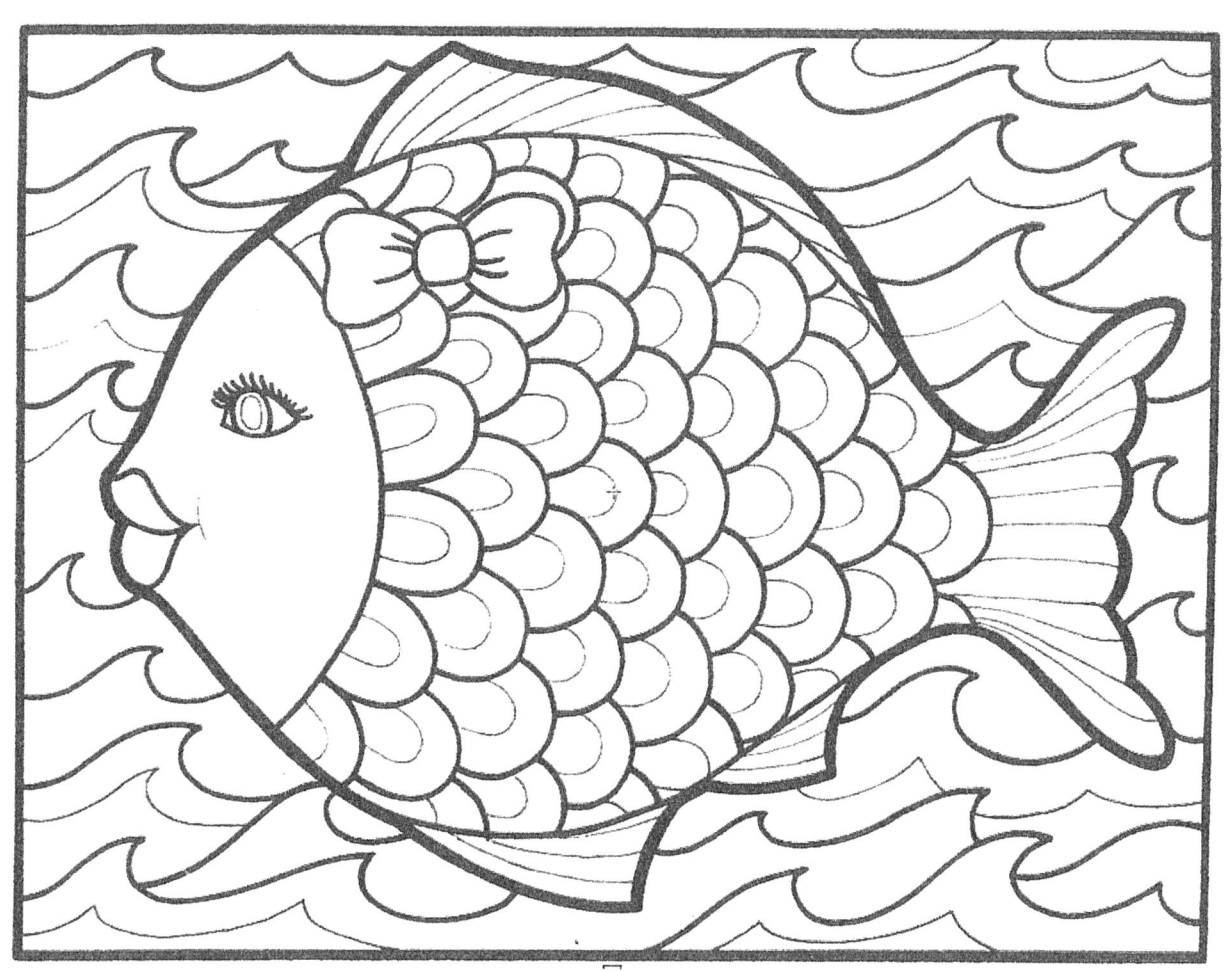

Do not speak about anyone who is not physically present.

A single thought can shift your entire world.

A single thought can shift your entire world.

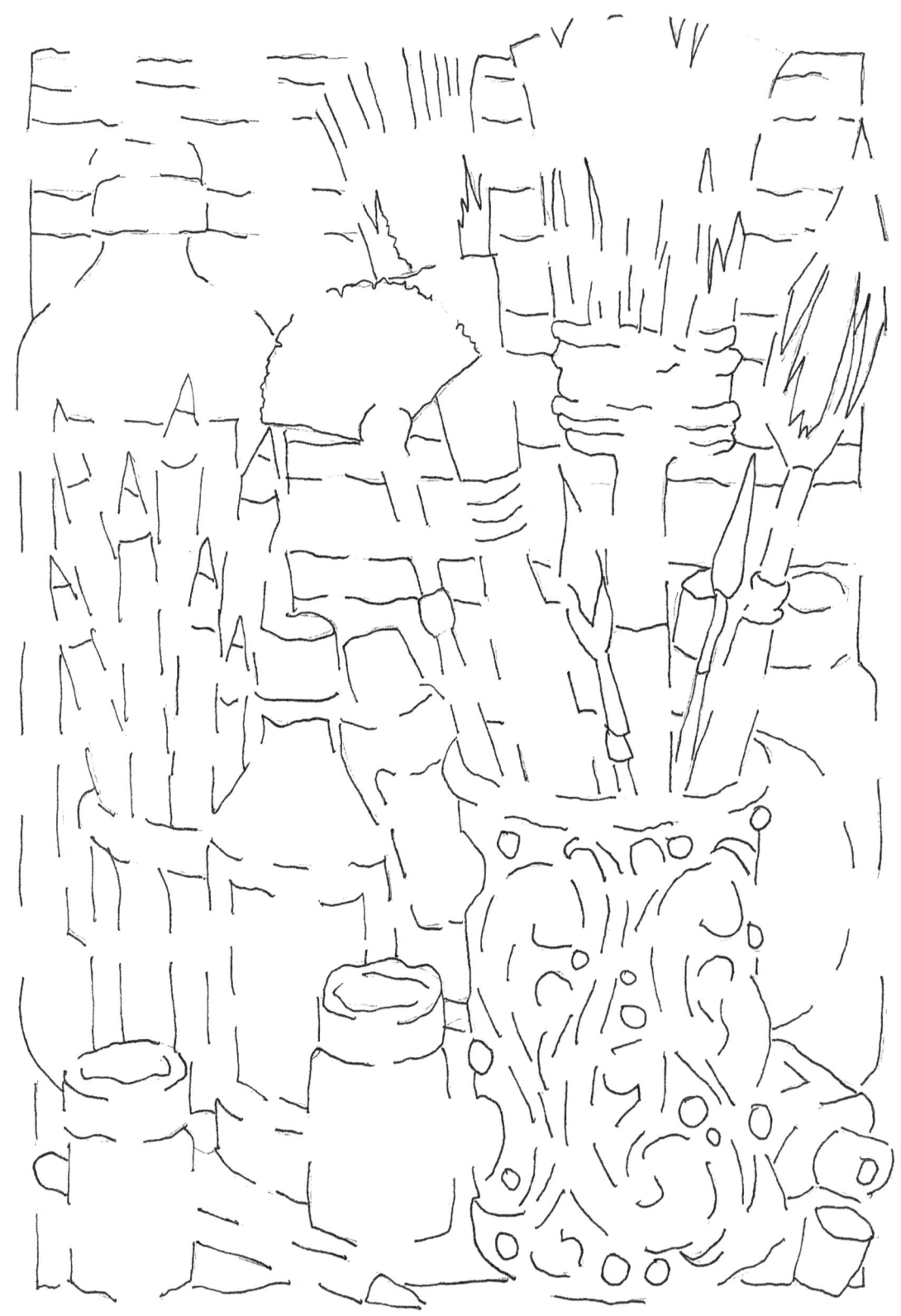

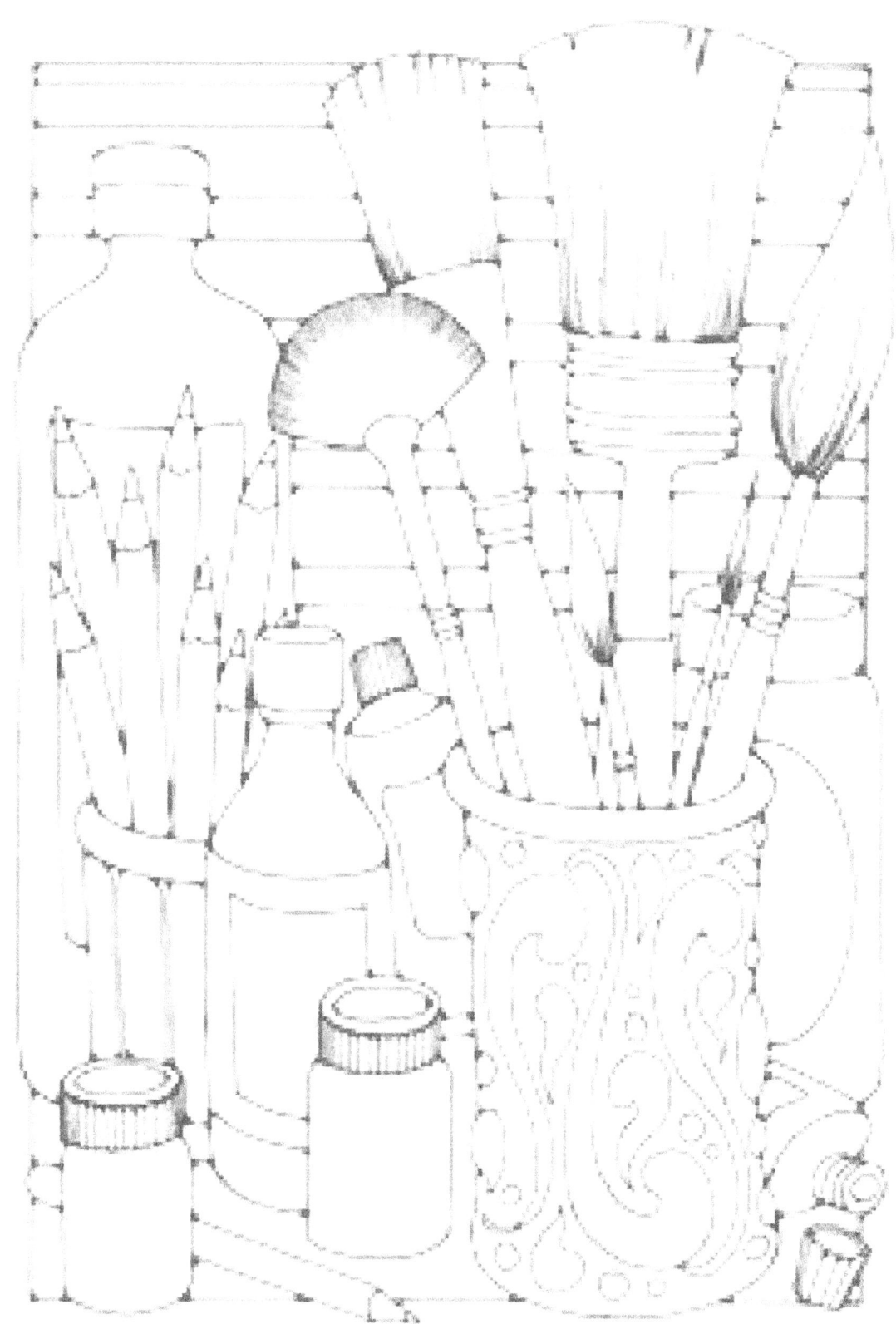

Your mind may trick you, but your heart never will.

As soon as we wish to be happier, we are no longer happy.

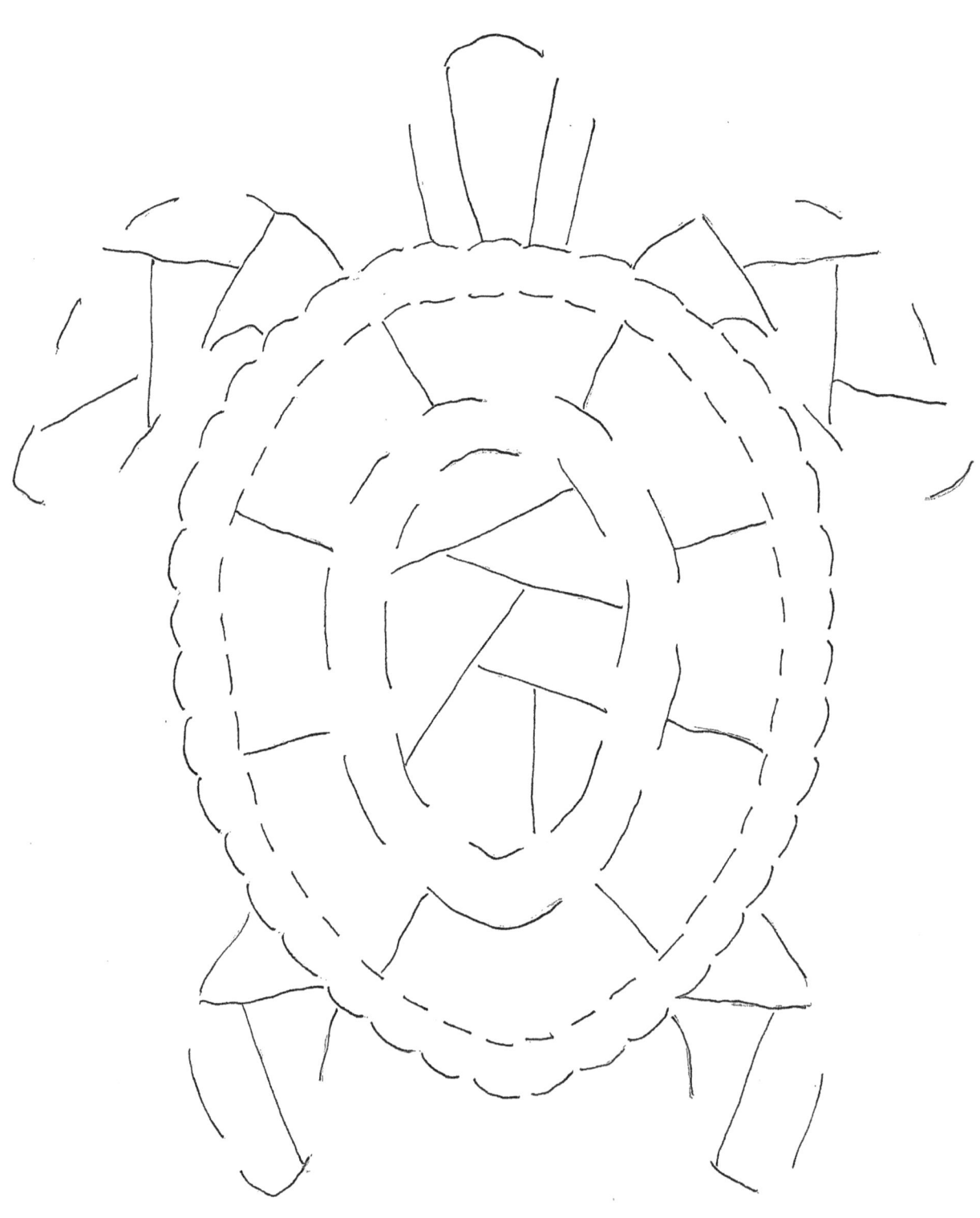

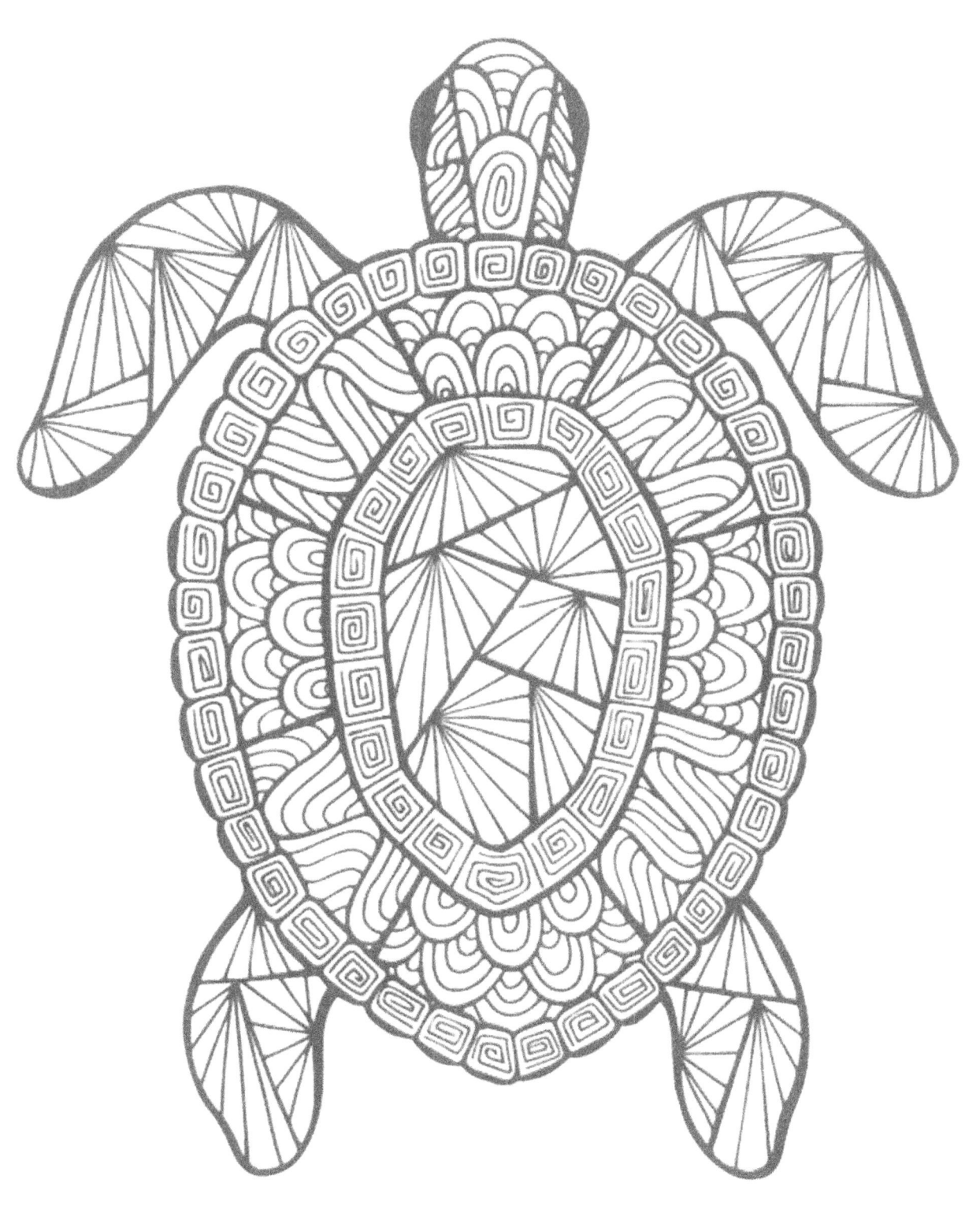

Observe the space between your thoughts, and then observe the observer.

Be kind whenever possible. It is always possible.

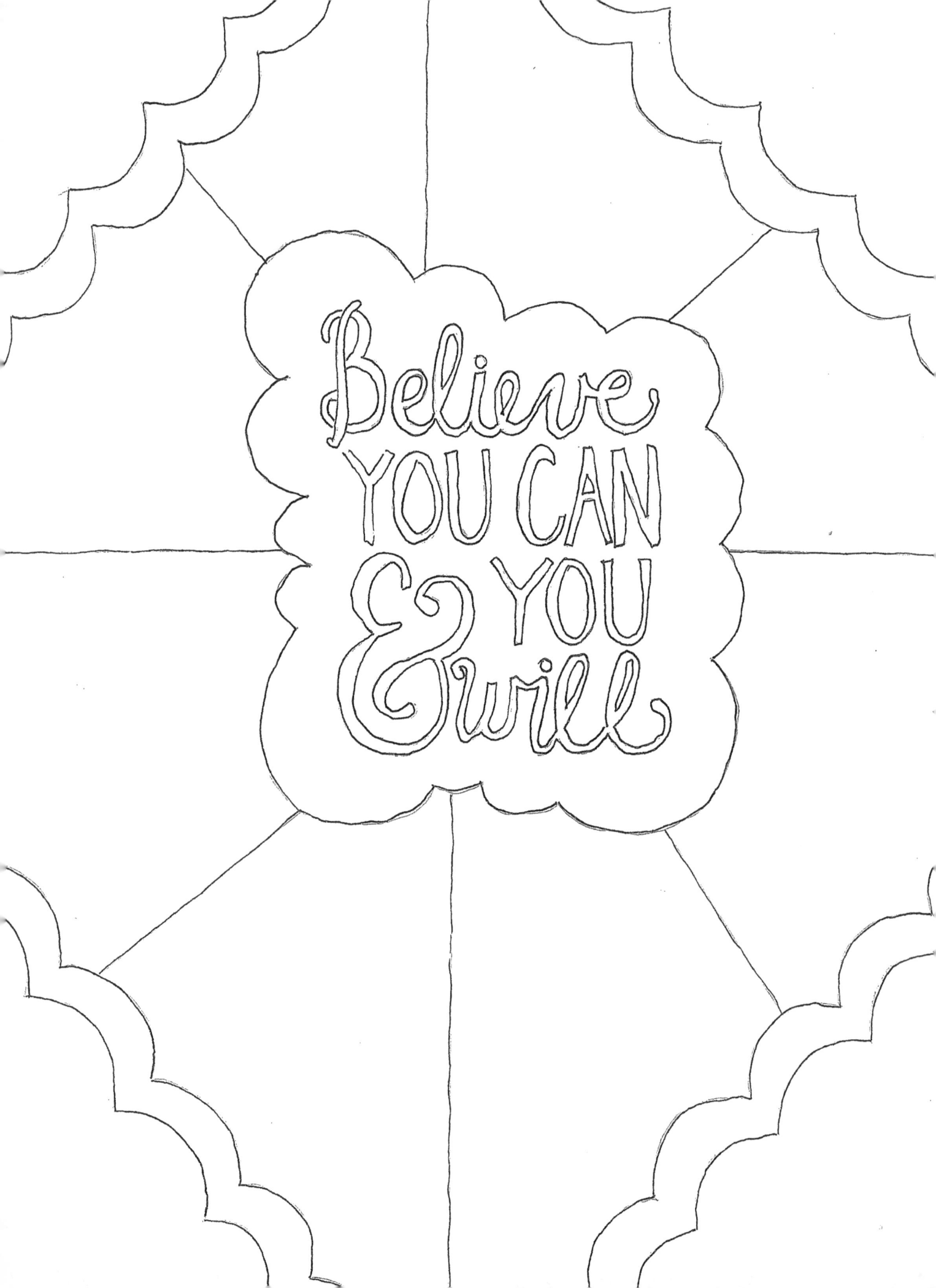

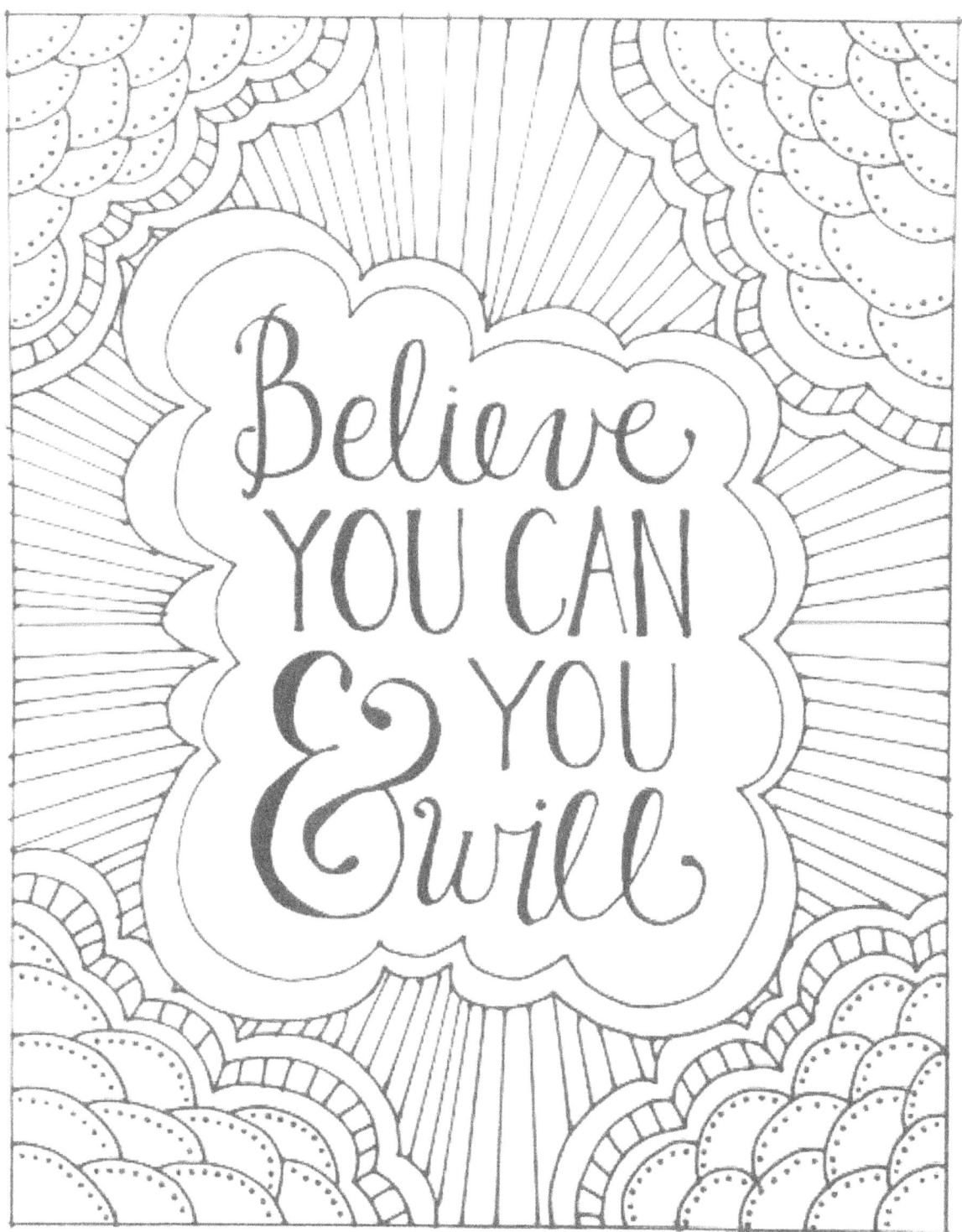

Do every act of your life as though it is the last act of your life.

Everything is created twice, first in the mind and then in reality.

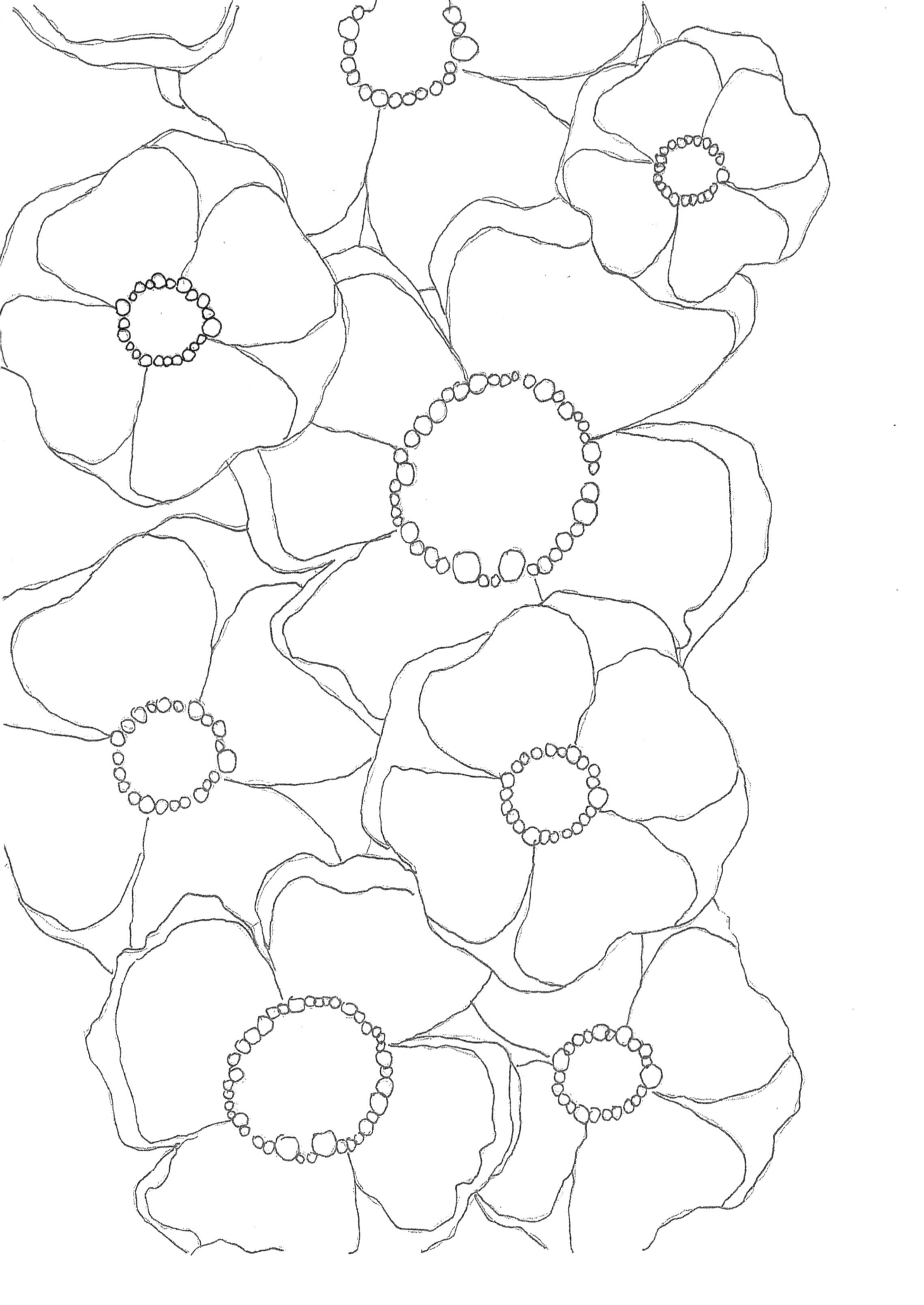

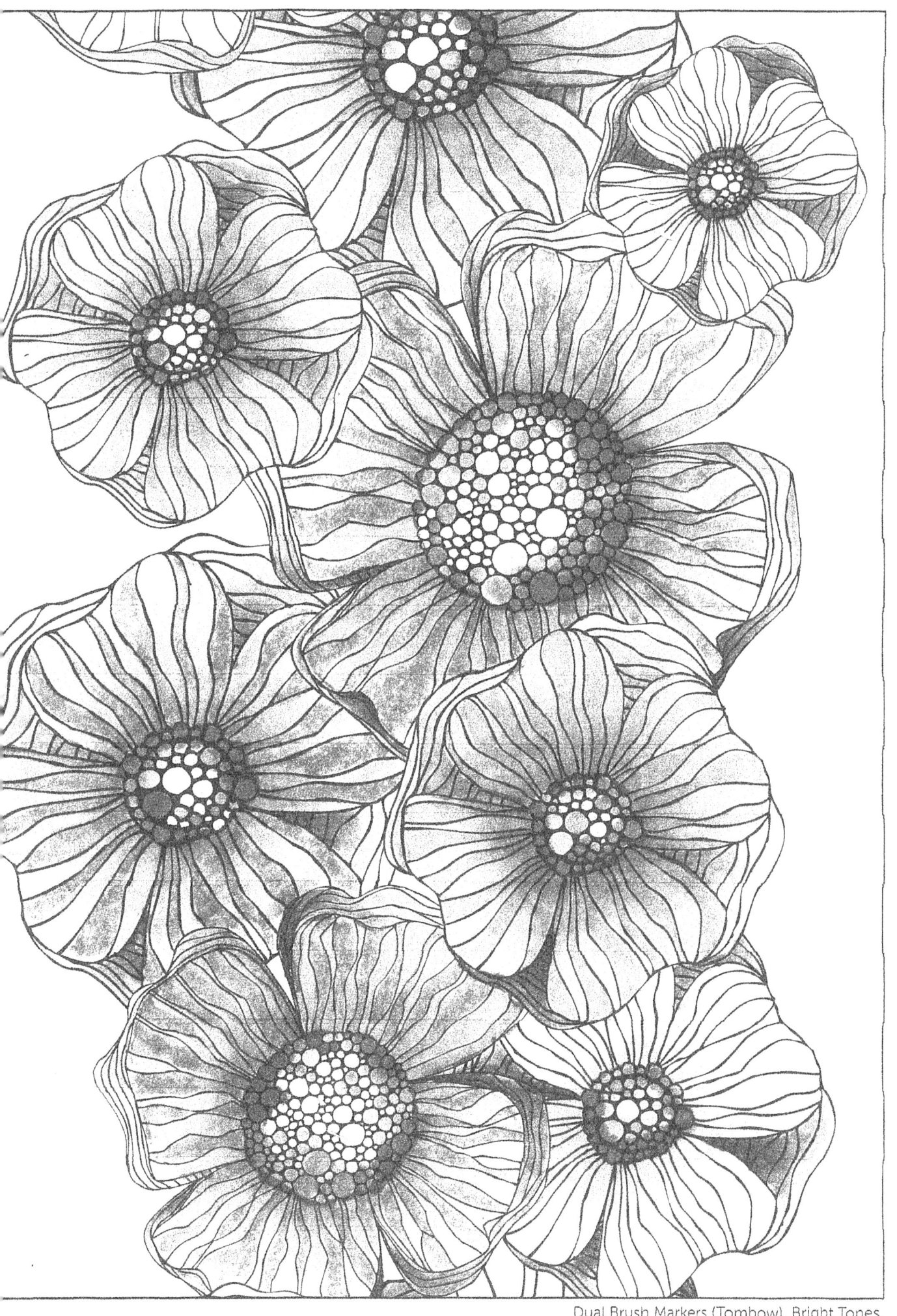
Dual Brush Markers (Tombow). Bright Tones.
Color by Marie Browning.

Walk as if you are kissing the earth with your feet.

Mindfulness is about a quiet mind, not able arriving, but being.

Mindfulness is about a quiet mind, not able arriving, but being.

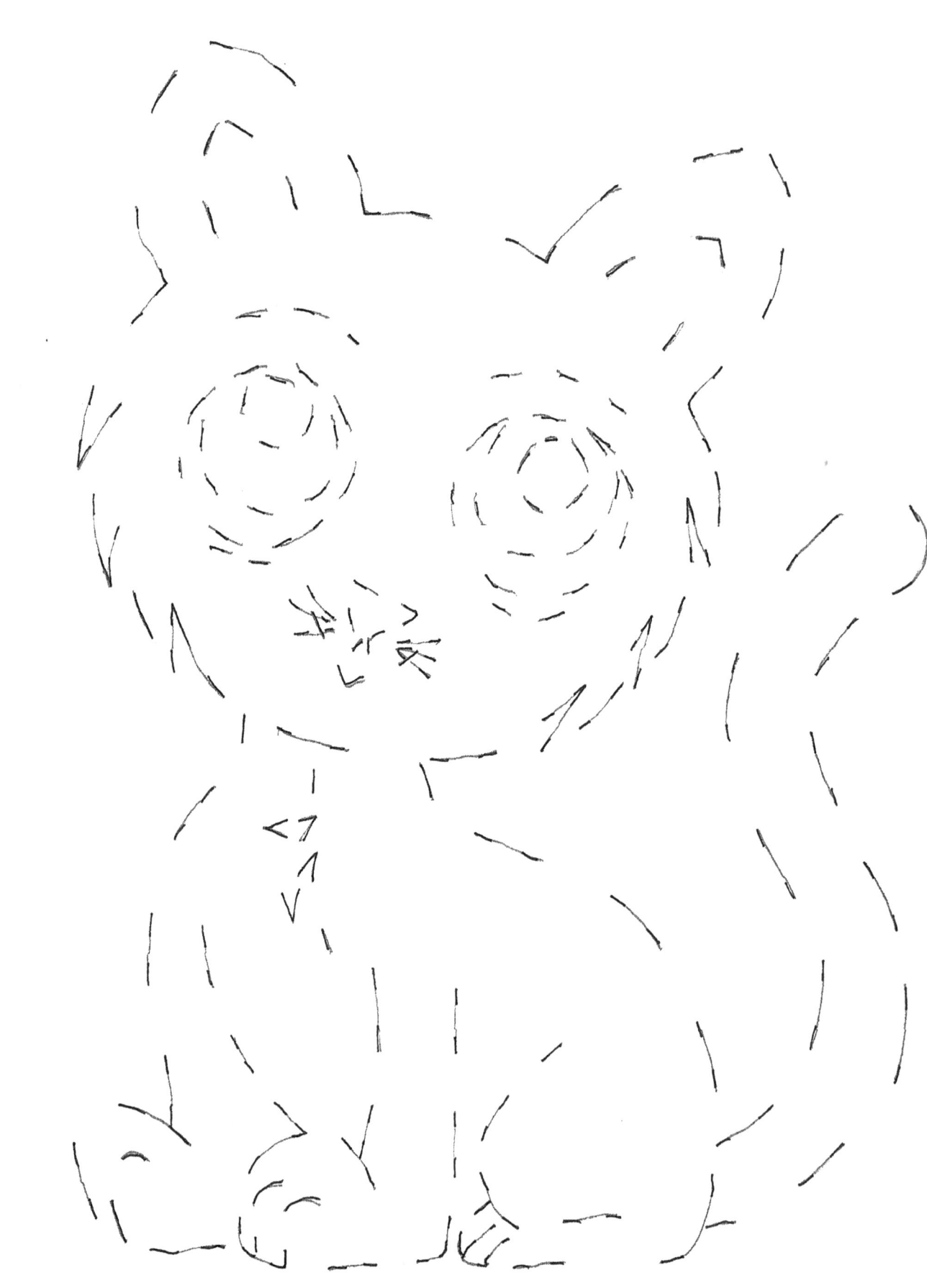

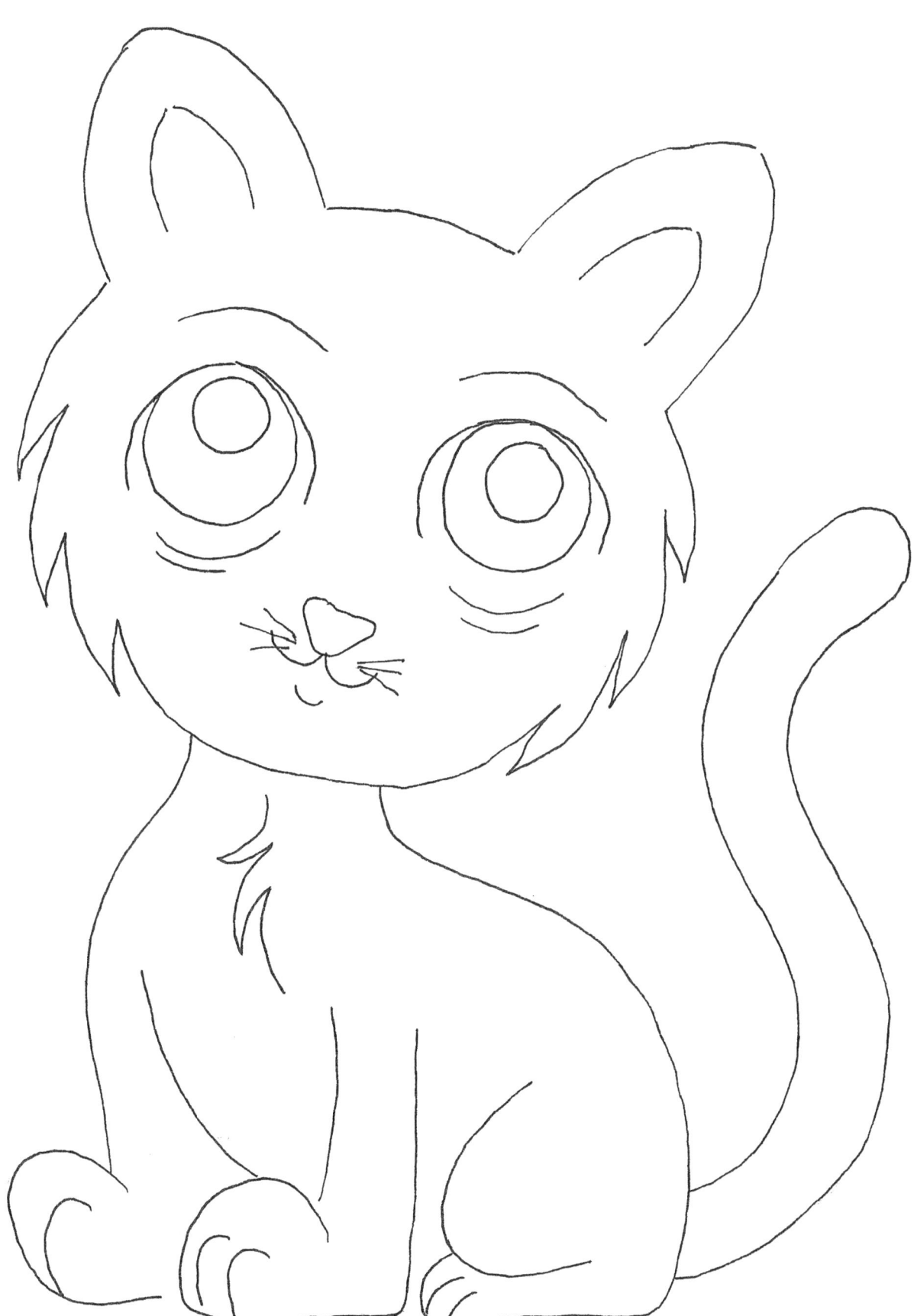

Everything is created twice, first in the mind and then in reality.

When all is said and done, beautiful moments are your true treasures.

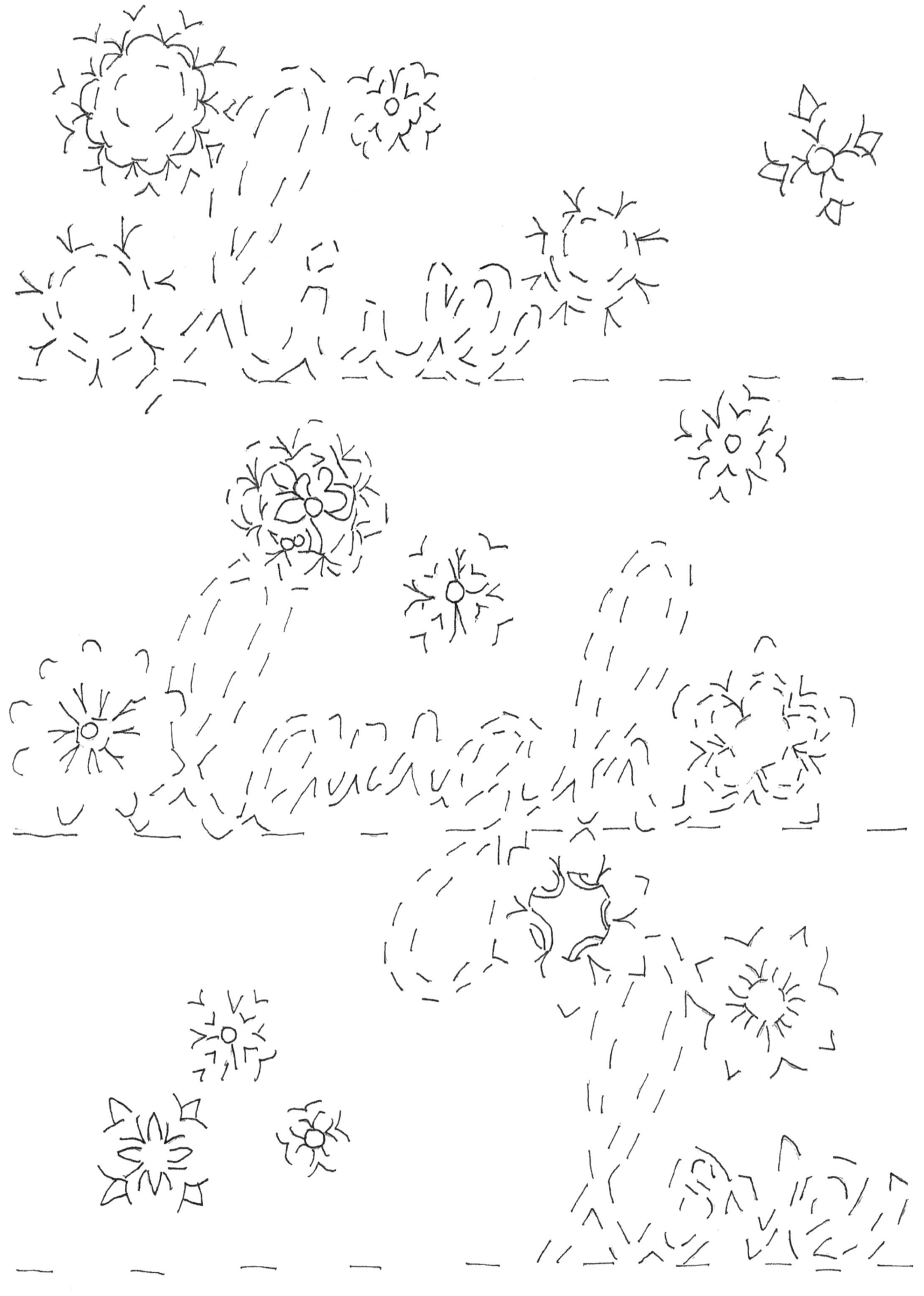

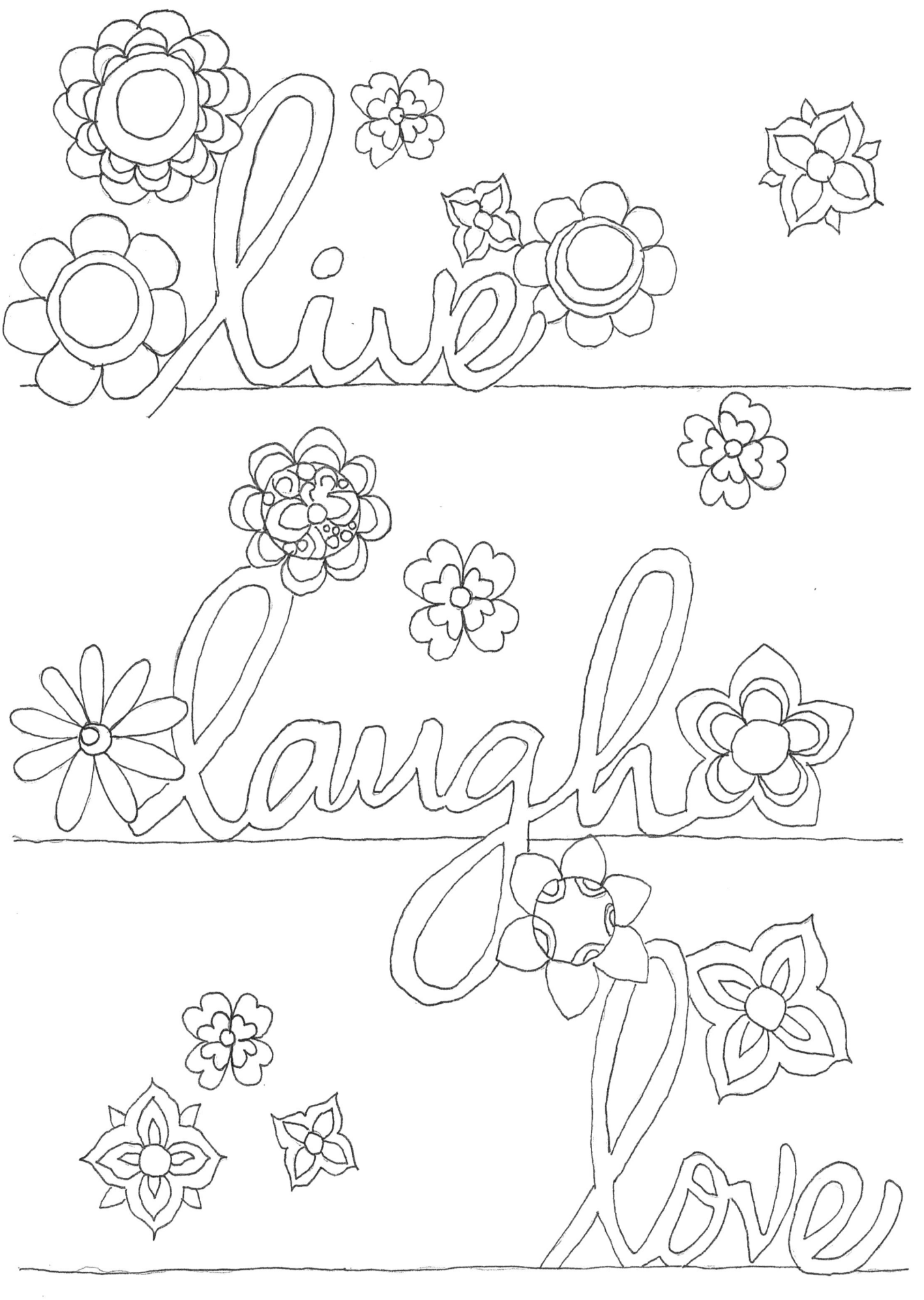

People cannot relate to a perfectionist, there is beauty in brokenness. Your story will bring healing to others.

www.ingramcontent.com/pod-product-compliance
Lightning Source LLC
Chambersburg PA
CBHW082357220526
45470CB00008B/2777